SOCIAL AMNESIA

SOCIAL AMNESIA

A Critique of Conformist Psychology
from Adler to Laing

by Russell Jacoby

Beacon Press   Boston

Introduction copyright © 1975 by Beacon Press
Beacon Press books are published under the auspices
of the Unitarian Universalist Association
First published as a Beacon Paperback in 1975
Printed in the United States of America

(hardcover)   9   8   7   6   5   4   3   2   1
(paperback)   9   8   7   6   5   4   3

Library of Congress Cataloging in Publication Data

Jacoby, Russell.
   Social amnesia.
   Includes bibliographical references and index.
   1.   Psychoanalysis — History.   I.   Title.
BF175.J3   335.43′8′15019509   74-16664
ISBN 0-8070-2964-5

Chapter V, "Politics of Subjectivity," appeared in slightly different
form in *Telos*, 9 (Fall 1971), and *New Left Review*, 79
(May–June 1973).

Contents

Introduction

Russell Jacoby is a historian, but his book is so far from being a conventional historical account of the development of psychoanalysis that many readers may not recognize it as the work of a historian at all. For one thing, it is openly polemical, not "objective." For another, it deals for the most part not with empirical questions but with questions of theory. Yet the theories to which it is addressed — psychoanalysis, Marxism, and the "critical theory" that tried to bring them together — are themselves deeply historical. Indeed they show more respect for the complexity and ambiguity of the past, and for the problematical character of historical interpretation, than much of the work of empirical historians, including those who have condemned these very theories as unhistorical.

At the same time, those theories keep constantly in mind the influence of the past on the present, in contrast to the enlightened view of the past, so popular nowadays, that treats the past as something safely left behind. Our present "enlightenment," according to Jacoby, is really a form of what he calls social amnesia, a willful repression of things we already knew. Thus we have chosen to "forget" psychoanalysis because it is disturbing — not least because it insists that the past is not so easily shuffled off as we suppose. The past "lives on," as Freud said, "in the ideologies of the super-ego and yields only slowly to the influences of the present and to new changes."

In an age that has forgotten theory, theory has to begin in remembrance. Jacoby's understanding of this central fact immediately distinguishes him from historians who write about psychoanalysis (and about the past in general) only in order to bury it still further. There is history that remembers and history that originates in a need to forget.

Historical treatments of psychoanalysis have usually been undertaken for one of two reasons: to "apply" psychoanalytic techniques to the solution of historical problems or to place the origins of the psychoanalytic movement in their "historical context."

The first type of work leads almost invariably to simplification and reductionalism. Psychoanalysis cannot be regarded as a tool-kit, which historians can delve into selectively as the need arises. It is a theory, and it has to be understood first of all in its own wholeness, secondly in relation to other theories offering contradictory or complementary interpretations of the world, and only thirdly (if at all) as a means of interpreting historical facts. Its implications, if firmly grasped, complicate the historian's work rather than simplify it. Instead of allowing the historian to reduce social, economic, and political phenomena to their psychological "roots," psychoanalysis forces him to consider the opposite movement as well: the social, economic, and political origins of psychic phenomena. To hold both of these "moments" simultaneously in view, however, is beyond the power of scholars working in the positivist tradition, so clearly the dominant intellectual tradition in the English-speaking world.

Many historians and students of society and culture welcome psychoanalysis as a technique that dispenses with the need for conventional historical analysis, indeed for thought of any kind, by providing an allegedly deeper understanding of political and religious movements; for example, by showing us that the Reformation, in the words of William L. Langer, sprang from a "mass emotional disturbance" and from pervasive feelings of guilt. When Langer urged the historical profession to undertake the study of psychoanalysis as "the next assignment" and cited the Reformation as an example of what psychoanalysis could do for history, he left the impression, perhaps unavoidably, that "emotional disturbances" were much more important than the religious issues the Reformation was ostensibly about. Deploring the pseudopsychoanalytic biographies of the twenties, which Langer complained had discredited psychohistory by identifying it with debunking — reducing a subject to his symptoms — Langer singled out as an alleged exception one of the most notorious examples of this genre, Preserved Smith's study of Luther, in which Luther is treated (I use the word advisedly) as "a thoroughly typical example of the neurotic quasi-historical sequence of an infantile sex-complex." [1]

One reason most of the work that falls under the heading of "psychohistory" has been simplistic and reductionist is that historians who have turned to Freud for help have not taken his ideas seriously enough to begin with. They have underestimated the intrinsic difficulty of those ideas and the effort needed to master them, satisfying themselves with superficial impressions, and confusing elements of Freud's thought with that of the neo-Freudians. Psychohistory has suffered from the amateurish, offhand approach that so many of its practitioners bring to the theory underlying it. Erik H. Erikson, noting that Preserved Smith, besides psychoanalyzing Luther, also wrote his biography and edited his letters, writes, "This paper ["Luther's Early Development in the Light of Psychoanalysis"] impresses one as being a foreign body in Smith's work on Luther; it is done, so to speak, with the left hand, while the right and official hand is unaware." [2] The same could be said of Langer, who made a reputation for solid, conventional political, and diplomatic history before discovering, in what one can only suppose was a rather casual and offhand way, the interpretive power of psychoanalysis. It is not altogether surprising that Erikson, a psychoanalyst, has written better history (whatever its theoretical implications) than historians who have dabbled in psychoanalysis — or for that matter than many of those who have immersed themselves in it.

For there is a deeper difficulty, namely that it is not only the ideas of *Freud* that historians do not take seriously.

It is an occupational hazard of what is called intellectual history that it often results in taking *no* ideas seriously. The fact of their historical origin, that is, is taken as evidence of their fallibility. Historical relativism — the nearest thing in this country to a philosophy of history — tells us that one idea is as good as another.

Intellectual historians, having usually made it their business to trace ideas to their historical origins, have a built-in bias, not only as relativists but as students of genesis, to see ideas as purely reflective and symptomatic. A thinker like Luther is no more exempt from this tendency than Freud himself. It may be because they find it difficult in the first place to understand how Luther could have broken with Rome over an *idea* that historians are tempted to attribute the break to his being "chronically oppressed by a pathological feeling of guilt," in Langer's words.

What is lacking, then, among practitioners of "psycho-history," is not only a mastery of psychoanalytic theory but, perhaps more important, the ability to perform an elementary act of historical imagination — to understand how the issues of the past appeared to the men of the time; to understand, for example (to refer to another study of Luther, that of Norman O. Brown), not only why it is important that "the Protestant illumination came to Luther while seated on the privy" but why it was important to Luther himself to record this fact.[3]

Intellectual history in the United States has been dominated by the historical relativism of Charles A. Beard and Carl Becker and more recently by the sociology of knowledge. The field became academically respectable only when it divorced itself, in the thirties, from the old-fashioned "history of ideas," which was accused, not without reason, of treating the development of ideas in a historical vacuum (as if ideas floated in a timeless void) and of ignoring the study of ideology. Under the influence of Becker and later of Mannheim, intellectual historians tried to put ideas into "historical context." Too often, however, this meant treating ideas as purely "responses" to immediate societal (or psychological) determinants — a procedure that always ends by trivializing ideas. This brings us to the second type of historical work on Freud — historical study of the psychoanalytic movement itself, which illustrates these tendencies very clearly.[4] The main thrust of that work has been to treat psychoanalysis as the product of a specific cultural milieu, that of Vienna at the turn of the century, or more broadly as part of a general reaction against positivism at the end of the nineteenth century. This approach serves, willy-nilly, to historicize away precisely what is most original and penetrating in Freudian theory. Freud is seen as a "man of his times," who overemphasized the sexual origins of neurosis because he lived in a sexually repressive society that was at the same time obsessed with sex, and who exaggerated the importance of biology because he inherited the mechanistic assumptions of nineteenth-century medicine and did not have access to our sophisticated understanding of the "cultural factor." It is tempting, in the face of this historical reductionism, to argue that historical understanding of Freud has to begin with loyalty to his basic concepts. At the very least it has to recognize that at the time those concepts were formulated, they represented for some thinkers the most promising attack on the most urgent questions facing Western society. It is in this sense, first of all and foremost of all, that psychoanalysis — or any other body of serious thought — has to be understood as "the product of its time."[5]

Jacoby is not particularly concerned, in the present study, with the historical origins of psychoanalysis; his subject is its subsequent development and perversion. His discussion of an analogous problem, however — the origin in the 1920s of what he calls "negative psychoanalysis" — shows a more profoundly historical understanding than the historical reductionism I have been criticizing — one that does not automatically diminish the ideas it examines. It arises, let it be noted, not out of a desire to be historically "objective" but out of an intense but by no means uncritical engagement with perspectives that developed in the twenties and thirties, notably with the work of Lukács and of the so-called Frankfurt School. The overriding intellectual problem confronting these thinkers, according to Jacoby, was the need to explain why bourgeois society had survived the revolutionary crisis of 1914–1919 — why the revolutionary movement had failed, in spite of the fact that the objective conditions for the collapse of capitalism (as Gramsci noted, along with many others) had been present for decades. As Western European Marxists pondered this question, they became conscious of the limits of a purely objective Marxism. What was missing from European society, it appeared, were the *subjective* conditions of social revolution; hence only a Marxism capable of analyzing subjectivity (instead of merely deducing it from economic "laws") was capable of analyzing the crisis of industrial society. This insight gave rise in turn to an interest in culture and ideology, the rediscovery of the early Marx, the new attention paid to the Hegelian roots of Marxism, and in general an attempt to revive the dialectical element in a Marxist tradition that had succumbed to positivism.[6]

Jacoby not only shows how the new interest in subjectivity made psychoanalysis relevant to Marxism, he suggests, to put it more strongly, that Marxists seeking to understand late bourgeois society ignored psychoanalysis at their peril. He indicates that the work of Lukács, for example, suffered because Lukács, for all his interest in subjectivity, refused to avail himself of Freud, and that the work of the Frankfurt School, on the other hand, was enriched at every point by the encounter with psychoanalysis. He then traces the transformation of psychoanalytic theory, ironically by men and women sympathetic to the left, who sought to humanize Freud and succeeded only in losing sight of the tension between theory and therapy. The result was a psychology that even in the more radical version of Laing and Cooper (which at least tried to revive Freud's insistence on the continuum between madness and sanity) consistently confused therapy with the reconstruction of society.

Jacoby does not emphasize the point, but it can be argued that one of the reasons for the "repression" of the critical elements in Freud's thought was that the center of psychoanalytic activity shifted, in the thirties (perhaps even as early as the twenties), from central Europe to England and the United States. The "forgetting" of Freud is closely allied to the translation of Freud, so to speak, into English — that is, the assimilation of psychoanalysis to positivism. Neither England nor the United States had an intellectual tradition comparable to the Hegelian-Marxian tradition, one capable of incorporating psychoanalysis in a way that would preserve its critical content. In the United States in particular the problem appeared to be not to explain why the revolution had failed but why, happily, it was unnecessary in the first place. Theories of American exceptionalism, with their usual optimistic overtones, prevented Americans from grasping the full implications of the First World War — namely that the left had suffered a disastrous defeat all over the Western world; that the American left was no exception; that capitalism had entered a new and more sinister phase in which its control over the individual would be greatly extended (partly because of the weakness of the left); and that these developments, finally, demanded a new understanding of the ways in which bourgeois hegemony was exercised — in short demanded, among other things, a critical psychology.[7] Not only the American left but Americans of all political persuasions remained confident, as always, that the United States could avoid the fate of Europe.

Randolph Bourne had glimpsed the truth in 1917 when he wrote that the United States had not made education its "national enterprise," as the progressives had hoped, but had chosen war instead. It was not Bourne, however, but his antagonist, John Dewey, who represented the American mainstream; nor was anything more characteristic of American thought than Dewey's continuing hope, long after the possibility of such a solution had ceased to exist (if it ever had), that the sickness of bourgeois society could be cured through education in humane values and "co-operation." It goes almost without saying that American social thought, with its essentially therapeutic outlook on the world, proved eminently receptive to the work of the Freudian revisionists and, later, to "humanist" psychology, which in Jacoby's words proposes not to destroy dehumanization but to humanize it.

The work of the Frankfurt School, even when its founders migrated to the United States and began to publish in English, made little impression on the American scene. Adorno's work was known almost exclusively through *The Authoritarian Personality,* which was mistaken for a purely psychological analysis of politics, notwithstanding Adorno's repeated warnings that "the subjectively oriented analyses have their value only within the objective theory" — that is, psychological analysis is insufficient without a theory that recognizes the psyche itself as the distillation of history.[8] But the misinterpretation of this work was less surprising, perhaps, than the fact that the Frankfurt School's work on mass culture made so little impression on the critique of mass culture being developed, in the forties and fifties, by Dwight Macdonald, Irving Howe, and other writers, mostly ex-Trotskyists, formerly associated with *Partisan Review.* These critics' insistence on the importance of cultural issues, their receptivity to psychoanalysis, and their contempt for the mechanical Marxism now doubly discredited by association with Stalinism, might have predisposed them to a sympathetic engagement with "critical theory." Instead the American critics of mass culture borrowed what they needed from the Europeans without attempting to master the theory on which the latter's work was based. Similarly in the sixties the New Left seized on the later works of Herbert Marcuse in order to justify its own ideas of cultural revolution, often without understanding Marcuse's connections to the Frankfurt School or the philosophical origins of his thought. "Critical theory," as Jacoby makes clear in his chapter on "The Politics of Subjectivity," does not support a regressive critique of capitalism based on "a new and repressive equality." Yet Marcuse remained a hero of the counter-culture until some of its spokesmen became uneasily aware of what, in their confusion, they denounced as the "elitist" drift of his thought.[9]

The defeat of the New Left gives added urgency to the questions raised by the Frankfurt School and by other Marxists in the twenties. The renewed interest in culture and the family, the revival of feminist activism, even the vogue of psychology, testify to a growing awareness of the inadequacy of a purely objective analysis of capitalism at the same time they reveal society's success in diverting political criticism to cultural issues that too often lead merely to harmless personal rebellion and so-called consciousness-raising. One of the main virtues of Jacoby's book is that it helps to identify what is useful and what is trivial and sentimental in the current preoccupation with culture and psychology. For this alone it should be welcomed and read.

There is a great deal more to say about the virtues of this book, but attentive readers will discover them for themselves — I trust with the same delight with which I have followed the development of this remarkable scholar.

Christopher Lasch

Avon, New York
June 1974

Preface

The intensive and extensive interest in psychology is too vast to characterize. Those who seek relief from a malaise in society as well as disenchanted radicals who seek an alternative to the impoverishment of past political praxis look to psychology; and this only begins the list. The very length and diversity of the list, however, if it resists characterization, suggest one conclusion: psychology is not a passing fad on the fringes of society; rather it is deeply entangled in the social reality. For this reason any study of psychology must simultaneously study the society and culture of which it is a part.

The shift in social attention toward psychology is no accident; it testifies to a shift in the social structure itself. In baldest terms, the individual psyche commands attention exactly because it is undergoing fragmentation and petrification; the living substance known as the individual is hardening. The autonomous ego — always problematic — proves to be no match for the social collectivity, which has at its call alternatively brute force, jobs, television, or the local newspaper. This is no conspiracy; rather it is ingrained in the *social* relations which both nourish and poison *human* relations. What haunts the living is the specter of individual and psychic suffocation; this is the specter that conformist psychology seeks to put to rest.

Within psychology new theories and therapies replace old ones at an accelerating rate. In a dynamic society, Freud is too old to be a fashion, too new to be a classic. The phenomenon of the newer replacing the new is not confined to psychology; it is true in all realms of thought. The new not only surpasses the old, but displaces and dislodges it. The ability as well as the desire to remember atrophies. Most of the social sciences turn radically ahistorical; one hardly studies Hegel within philosophy, Freud within psychology, Marx within economics, and so on.

For some, this is proof of progress and vitality. But dynamism can be perpetual motion without forward movement. Within the dynamism a static moment can inhere: the structure of society. The evident acceleration of production and consumption in the economic sphere, and hysteria and frenzy in life itself, does not preclude that a fixed society is simply spinning faster. If this is true, the application of planned obsolescence to thought itself has the same merit as its application to consumer goods; the new is not only shoddier than the old, it fuels an obsolete social system that staves off its replacement by manufacturing the illusion that it is perpetually new.

This book is an effort to remember what is perpetually lost under the pressure of society; it bucks the planned obsolescence of thought. It does not, however, intend to be archeology, the mere uncovering of what is lost. It is simultaneously a critique of present practices and theories in psychology. As a *critique* it renounces the positivist schema that neatly severs facts from values, observation from thought. Hence the following is both analysis and polemic because they are inseparable. A critique in the Marxist tradition rests on a notion of truth that resists mindless tolerance; all ideas are not equally true, and hence not all are equally tolerable. To tolerate them all is to degrade each one. At least in the realm of ideas the notion of consensus and harmony is unacceptable. "Pure" tolerance is, in any case, to follow Marcuse, sullied to the core. The free market of ideas has never been free, but always a market. To undo this necessitates not commissars and censors but critical intelligence loyal to an objective notion of truth. If there **is** repressive tolerance, then there is also liberating intolerance.[1] "Truth cannot be tolerant," wrote Freud.[2]

The critique of sham innovation in psychology and the planned obsolescence of thought cannot in turn endorse the blind repetition of the old and the past: the collecting of antiques. In psychology, as elsewhere, there is never a lack of those content to repeat the words of their teachers — here be it Freud, there be it Marx — as if nothing has changed in the interim. Something has changed in the interim, and the concepts, if they are not to congeal into meaningless symbols, must themselves change to remain adequate to a historical reality.

This question is discussed in Chapter I; however one aspect must be mentioned here. The formulating of concepts that avoid a phony originality or witless repetition obviously has a bearing on words and language. The very words used to describe this society either overshoot it or lag behind it. Designations such as "industrial" or "post-industrial" society are fashionable; they suggest the historic alternatives of capitalism and socialism have been left behind by a technological structure that is universal and inescapable.[3] The reverse, "bourgeois" society, and the like, imply that nothing has changed since Marx and Engels wrote. If the former is apologetic, the latter tends to be blind in its critique. Yet the latter, at least, refers to certain structural elements of society that are not technological, but historical, that is, subject to change and choice. There is no satisfying solution; hence in this book there is no flight from the use of words such as "bourgeois," but neither will they be relentlessly attached to every noun. But let there be no doubt: the concepts of "society," "thought," "life," and so on, do not exist outside and beyond history; they are located within a social reality. If not always stated, in question here are the nonsocialist industrialized countries of Western Europe and North America; they are rooted in capitalism, and have yet to transcend it.

A few preliminary clarifications and definitions are necessary: The Frankfurt School is an informal term for the collective thought of a group of Marxist thinkers who formulated in Frankfurt, Germany, prior to Hitler, and then in exile, a theory known as "critical theory" or "critical theory of society." In the Anglo-American world, Herbert Marcuse remains the best known of the Frankfurt School, but of equal importance are Theodor W. Adorno and Max Horkheimer.[4] Of the Frankfurt School writings, this book is essentially concerned with its critique of the neo-Freudians, and will neglect theoretical differences, sometimes considerable, between Frankfurt School members; furthermore, discussion will be deferred on the more recent contributions of the Frankfurt School, including those by Jürgen Habermas, the late Max Horkheimer, and others.

"Neo-Freudians" refers essentially to Erich Fromm, Karen Horney, Clara Thompson, and Harry S. Sullivan. While Fromm on occasion decries this label, it seems advisable to retain it. These thinkers are united not only because they were associated at one time, but because they share a critique of Freud and a psychology that converges on several important elements. Because of their emphasis on the role of culture and interpersonal relations they are also known as the "cultural interpersonal school." There are evident parallels between this school of thought and what in England is called the "object-relations theory."[5] Within this book Sullivan and Thompson are the least, and Fromm the most, important.

Post-Freudians is not a satisfactory term; but it has received certain usage and is difficult to replace; it refers to a loose collection of thinkers such as Abraham Maslow, Gordon Allport, Carl Rogers. They, unlike the neo-Freudians, do not emerge from a psychoanalytic framework. Rather their roots are in a personal, counseling, existential psychological tradition that has distanced itself from both behaviorism and psychoanalysis; they sometimes refer to themselves as humanist, existential, or "third force" psychologists; the latter refers to a place between psychoanalysis and behaviorism.

The following chapters pursue, at first, the forgetting of psychoanalysis and the emergence of a new ideology of liberation — a conformist psychology. Chapter I attempts to situate this phenomenon within a general cultural trend of social amnesia; further, it broaches some of the crucial concepts: revisionism and orthodoxy, theory and therapy. Chapter II takes a brief historical look at Alfred Adler, the first "revisionist," and his dispute with Freud; then considers some of the issues between the Frankfurt School and the neo-Freudians. It should be noted that no history of psychoanalysis is intended; only the recounting of certain elements. Chapter III subjects to criticism the post-Freudian psychology as conformist. Only a word is said on the behaviorists; not because they are less conformist but more — and rarely claim anything else; they stand within a narrow positivist tradition, and have, in the context of this book, less political significance.

Chapter IV pursues the relationship between psychoanalysis and Marxism; it seeks to trace some of the history and content of the Marx-Freud exchange, and attempts to formulate a notion of negative psychoanalysis or a nonsubjective theory of subjectivity. To minds schooled in pragmatism and common sense, these are alien concepts — but this is an alien world. That is the sole justification for their use. Again it should be noted that the treatment of psychoanalysis and Marxism does not intend to be exhaustive; it is selective in time and place. Notably left out are recent contributors in Germany, such as Alexander Mitscherlich, Alfred Lorenzer, et al., or those in France, such as Jacques Lacan, Gilles Deleuze, and Félix Guattari. The final chapters V–VII explore the place of subjectivity and the dangers of subjective reductionism both for a political left and for the radical psychology of R. D. Laing and David Cooper. The dialectic and divergence of theory and therapy are discussed as crucial to a negative and political psychology.

A preliminary note on these "alien" concepts. The neo- and post-Freudians blithely imagine they are adding "the self," "the person," "the individual" — subjectivity — to impersonal psychologies and a depersonalized reality. Yet to critical theory this appended subjectivity is ideological, false consciousness. The prevailing subjectivity is no oasis in a barren and dehumanized society; rather it is structured down to its core by the very society it fantasizes it left behind. To accept subjectivity as it exists today, or better, as it does not exist today, is implicitly to accept the social order that mutilates it. The point, however, is not merely to reject subjectivity in the name of science or affirm it in the name of poetry; it is to delve into subjectivity seriously. This seriousness entails understanding to what extent the prevailing subjectivity is wounded and maimed; such understanding means sinking into subjectivity not so as to praise its depths and profundity, but to appraise the damage; it means searching out the objective social conᵢ̣gurations that suppress and oppress the subject. Only in this way can subjectivity ever be realized: by understanding to what extent today it is objectively stunted. This is a notion that could be called an objective (or nonsubjective) theory of subjectivity.

It should be mentioned that the history of works that have drawn upon both psychoanalysis and Marxism has not been a happy one; it has generally taken the form of sectarian attacks, with Marxists claiming that psychoanalysis is idealistic and subjective, and psychoanalysts claiming that Marxism is a personal neurosis. The works sympathetic to both have generally succumbed to simplifications of either Marxism or psychoanalysis; this continual failure is probably due to the intellectual division of labor. Those who learn to master categories of political economy and philosophy have been unable to faithfully follow concepts of another kind, individual and psychic ones; and those adept in psychological concepts tend to be unschooled in social ones.

It would be brash to claim that there is nothing more urgent than to work out a relationship between psychology and a social theory; similarly it would be exaggerated but not false to state that without a psychological component Marxism degenerates into abstractions and irrelevant dogma; or that without a theoretical and social content psychology erodes into a technique. There are many urgent things to do, and many more urgent than this. Yet the pursuit of these issues is an integral part of the theory and praxis of liberation: social *and* human transformation.

Solidarity of two friends in particular has sustained and helped me through times thick and thin of thinking, writing, and living this book; to Naomi Glauberman and Paul Breines for their theoretical, moral, and loving aid, my grateful thanks. Irreplaceable solidarity has also come from those who generously read all or parts of the manuscript and gave me their support, their comments, their disagreements; at least Stanley Aronowitz, Joel Kovel, Christopher Lasch, Herbert Marcuse, and Howard Zinn should be mentioned and thanked. Finally, I wish to thank Wini Breines, Eliott Eisenberg, Marla Erlien, Robert Meyer, Jim Schmidt and other friends for their active interest, encouragement, and theoretical advice.

I

Social Amnesia and the New Ideologues

The history of philosophy is the history of forgetting: so
T. W. Adorno has remarked. Problems and ideas once examined fall out of sight and out of mind only to resurface
later as novel and new. If anything the process seems to be
intensifying; society remembers less and less faster and
faster. The sign of the times is thought that has succumbed
to fashion; it scorns the past as antiquated while touting
the present as the best. Psychology is hardly exempt. What
was known to Freud, half-remembered by the neo-Freudians, is unknown to their successors. The forgetfulness itself
is driven by an unshakable belief in progress: what comes
later is necessarily better than what came before. Today,
without romanticizing the past, one could almost state the
reverse: what is new is worse than what is old.

The celebration of the present is aided by instant history. Today's banalities apparently gain in profundity if
one states that the wisdom of the past, for all its virtues,
belongs to the past. The arrogance of those who come later
preens itself with the notion that the past is dead and gone.
Few can resist introducing stock criticism of Freud — be it
of the left or right — without the standard observation that
Freud was a nineteenth-century Viennese. The endless
repetition of such statements suggests the decline of critical thinking; the modern mind can no longer think thought,
only can locate it in time and space. The activity of thinking decays to the passivity of classifying. Freud is explained
away by positioning him in a nineteenth-century Vienna.
Today, bred and fed on twentieth-century urbane and liberal feed, we have apparently left behind history itself and
can view the past with the pleasure of knowing that we are

1

no longer part of it. Yet little bears the imprint of the present historical period more than this fake historical consciousness: the argument that past thought is past because it is past is a transparent alibi for the present. To accuse such reasoning with its own logic, it is the contemporary form of relativism; debased sociology of knowledge seeks to avoid thought by mechanically matching it with specific social strata and historical eras. Its awareness of historical transformation ideologically stops short of itself; its own viewpoint is considered neutral and absolute truth, outside — not inside — history.

The critique of Freud as hopelessly situated in Vienna and the nineteenth century unites cultural anthropologists, neo-Freudians, and theoreticians of women's liberation. Aside from those who joyfully or maliciously rewrite history and have it that Freud was merely the vanguard of the sexual mythology of his time — or worse[1] — it is repeated endlessly that he was a genius, but like all geniuses bound and blinded by his era. "Not even a genius," wrote Karen Horney of Freud, "can entirely step out of his time."[2] He was part of his era in that "in the nineteenth century there was little knowledge regarding cultural differences." Freud ascribed to biology what today we know is due to "culture." Or as Clara Thompson wrote, "Although a genius, Freud was in many respects limited by the thinking of his time, as even a genius must be." Specifically, "Much which Freud believed to be biological has been shown by modern research to be a reaction to a certain type of culture."[3] Patrick Mullahy wrote, "Freud could not surmount certain limitations of his culture and of his own nature. This was inevitable. Even a genius can do only so much." In particular, "Freud's intellectual framework, his whole orientation ... is a mechanistic-materialistic one. ... Freud grew up in the second half of the nineteenth century when scientific men generally espoused a philosophy of mechanistic-materialism."[4] Or more recently, Betty Friedan remarked of Freud that "even his genius could not give him, then, the knowledge of cultural processes" which is common knowledge today.[5]

It should be noted that the recent insight that psychoanalysis is a product of nineteenth-century Vienna is as recent as 1914, when it was already old. Freud wrote then:

> We have all heard the interesting attempt to explain psychoanalysis as a product of the peculiar character of Vienna as a city. . . . This inspiration runs as follows: psychoanalysis, so far as it consists of the assertion that the neuroses are traceable to disturbances in the sexual life, could only have come to birth in a town like Vienna . . . and it simply contains a reflection, a projection into theory, as it were, of these peculiar Viennese conditions. Now honestly I am no local patriot; but this theory about psychoanalysis always seems to me quite exceptionally stupid.[6]

Further, Freud glimpsed the future in which calling him a genius would be the password for easing him into the clubhouse of common sense. He is recorded as saying, "Calling me a genius is the latest way people have of starting their criticism of me. . . . First they call me a genius and then they proceed to reject all my views." [7]

Today criticism that shelves the old in the name of the new forms part of the *Zeitgeist;* it works to justify and defend by forgetting. In making only a fleeting gesture toward the past, or none at all, social and psychological thought turn apologetic. The heroic period of militant, materialistic, and enlightened bourgeois thought, if there ever was one, is no more. The "law" once enunciated on "the dwindling force of cognition in bourgeois society" can be confirmed daily.[8] In the name of a new era past theory is declared honorable but feeble; one can lay aside Freud and Marx — or appreciate their limitations — and pick up the latest at the drive-in window of thought.

The syndrome is a general one. In brief, society has lost its memory, and with it, its mind. The inability or refusal to think back takes its toll in the inability to think. The loss of memory assumes a multitude of forms, from a "radical" empiricism and positivism that unloads past thought like so much "intellectual baggage" to hip theories that salute the giants and geniuses of the past as unfortunates born too soon. The latter, more important in the context of this book, in the impatience to contrive new and novel theories, hustle through the past as if it were the junk yard of wrecked ideas. "In every era," wrote Walter Benjamin, "the attempt must be made to wrest tradition away from a conformism that is about to overcome it."

The general loss of memory is not to be explained solely psychologically; it is not simply childhood amnesia. Rather it is *social* amnesia — memory driven out of mind by the social and economic dynamic of this society. The nature of the production of social amnesia can barely be suggested here; such an explanation would have to draw upon the Marxist concept of reification. Reification in Marxism refers to an illusion that is objectively manufactured by society. This social illusion works to preserve the status quo by presenting the human and social relationships of society as natural — and unchangeable — relations between things. What is often ignored in expositions of the concept of reification is the psychological dimension: amnesia — a forgetting and repression of the human and social activity that makes and can remake society. The social loss of memory is a type of reification — better: it is *the* primal form of reification. "All reification is a forgetting." [9]

To pursue this for a moment: this form of reification is rooted in the necessities of the economic system. The intensification of the drive for surplus value and profit accelerates the rate at which past goods are liquidated to make way for new goods; planned obsolescence is everywhere, from consumer goods to thinking to sexuality. Built-in obsolescence exempts neither thought nor humans. What is heralded as new or young in things, thoughts, or people masks the constant: this society. Inherent in Marxism is the notion that dead labor dominates living, things dominate activity, the past commands the present. "The domination of capitalist over workers is the domination of things over men, dead labor over the living, products over producers. . . ." [10] Exactly because the past is forgotten, it rules unchallenged; to be transcended it must first be remembered. Social amnesia is society's repression of remembrance — society's own past. It is a psychic commodity of the commodity society.

The point here, though, is not to pursue an economic analysis; rather it is to excavate the critical and historical concepts that have fallen prey to the dynamic of a society that strips them both of their historical *and* critical content. In losing this content they turn apologetic or ideological. There is an irony here which is part of the problem: one of the very concepts formulated so as to comprehend this social process has succumbed to it: the concept of ideology. The concept of ideology is of double interest, both because the concept is used in these pages in its (partially) lost meaning and because an examination of its meaning is itself a short lesson in the process and effect of social forgetting. Some fifteen years ago Daniel Bell resuscitated the concept in *The End of Ideology* with the intent of burying it for good. He too discovered that the past was dead and gone; "ideology" was obsolete. "The old politico-economic radicalism . . . has lost its meaning. . . ." Now "in the western world . . . there is a rough consensus among intellectuals on political issues. . . ." [11]

Bell himself was well aware that the concept of ideology possessed a distinct content and history. But his account of the history of the concept was a formal exercise; it stood in no relation to his own definitions. With Bell, as with others such as Hannah Arendt, ideology is associated with abstract sloganeering, political passion, and violence; and it is contrasted with nonviolent, good-natured empiricism and pragmatism. "Ideology makes it unnecessary for people to confront individual issues on their individual merits," writes Bell; "Suffused by apocalyptic fervor, ideas become weapons, and with dreadful results."

The method rather to be followed must be "an empirical one." Arendt's argument is summed up in a chapter titled "Ideology and Terror" in her basic text of the cold war, *Origins of Totalitarianism*. Arendt links ideology with violence and evil, and contrasts it with common sense and empiricism. Ideologies are "isms which to the satisfaction of their adherents can explain everything and every occurrence by deducing it from a single premise." [12] Ideologies claim "total explanation," "independent of all experience." "All ideologies contain totalitarian elements." In the concluding section of the main part of her book, she tells us that the "aggressiveness of totalitarianism springs not from lust for power ... nor for profit ... but only for ideological reasons: to make the world consistent, to prove that its respective supersense has been right." [13]

Several things could be said about these formulations: the first, that they have been highly successful; they are deeply ingrained in the liberal consciousness which is convinced that ideology is a form of abstract nonempirical logic that issues into violence and terror. Secondly, despite the pretense of scholarship, they are false. The history of the concept of ideology has recently been told and need not be recounted here.[14] It must suffice to recall that ideology, aside from its factual origins in the *idéologues* of the French Revolution, derives from Marx. Crucial in this context is that in Marxism ideology is in no way restricted to what in Anglo-American tradition is considered abstract thought; rather it refers to a *form* of consciousness: *false* consciousness, a consciousness that has been falsified by social and material conditions. As a form of consciousness it could include *any* type of knowledge — idealism, empiricism, or positivism. Indeed, the latter was considered the ideology par excellence of the bourgeois market and culture: England. What determined if a consciousness was "false" was not an a priori categorizing of the type of knowledge, but an examination of its truth: its relationship to the concrete social reality.

The relevant point here is that the original Marxist notion of ideology was conveniently forgotten because it inconveniently did not exempt common sense and empiricism from the charge of ideology. The subsequent theory of ideology was directed solely against theoretical and philosophical concepts — concepts which could possibly defy common sense and empirical reality. Such concepts, not by chance, are inseparable from a radical social analysis. Dubbed "ideology" and saddled with all the ills of "totalitarianism," they are contrasted with a healthy and godly common sense that harms no living things. "Ideologies," Arendt tells us, "are never interested in the miracle of being," as if the miracle ingredient of the no-nonsense logic of the market were love itself. This argument promoted the pragmatic and antitheoretical consciousness already suspicious of theory and philosophy. The irony is that the Marxist notion of ideology was originally directed toward elucidating and articulating consciousness. But picked up by the practitioners of the sociology of knowledge and purged of its critical elements, it effected the "sabotage of consciousness" and not its restoration.[15] With Bell, Arendt, and a host of others its meaning was repressed, and a conformist one, openly or implicitly celebrating the common sense of the "West," was introduced.

The domestication and social repression of critical concepts such as ideology is the formula on which influential recent works — Alvin Toffler's *Future Shock,* Theodor Roszak's *The Making of a Counter Culture* — are built. They are marked by a refusal or inability to theorize in the name of a new era that has left behind traditional political categories. More exactly, new theories are advanced — "end of ideology," "future shock," "counter-culture" — but these turn out to be substanceless inasmuch as they are constructed out of only a sham confrontation with past theory. In their anxiety to leave behind the dated past they unwittingly fall into it, advancing new labels for old ideas. *Future Shock* can be considered the theoretical defense of this mode of operation, as well as its refutation. Its argu-

ment that each new item on the capitalist counter is a
shocking addition to freedom is contradicted by the book
itself, a drab repackaging of old apologetics. The reduction
of social antagonism and misery to a maladjustment between people and technology is an old approach; technology in this scheme exists in a no man's land, beyond
profit and exploitation. Technology "accelerates," Toffler
tells us, because it "feeds upon itself." "The supreme question which confronts our generation today — the question
to which all other problems are merely corollaries — is
whether technology can be brought under control," is Toffler's thesis as anticipated by the Rockefeller Foundation
Review of 1943.[16] The sleight of hand involves shifting attention from the social-economic structure to supposedly
neutral territory, as if today no one controls technology.
Such an analysis permits enough pathos to creep in to make
an enthusiasm for capitalism such as Toffler's acceptable to
those who rightly think that something is seriously wrong.

Roszak's analysis is made of the same stuff, though to
be sure it is more critical than Toffler's barely disguised
apologetics.[17] With the others he dismisses "the vintage rhetoric of radicalism." "Where the old categories of social
analysis have so little to tell us . . . it becomes a positive
advantage to confront the novelty of . . . politics free of
outmoded ideological preconceptions." Like Toffler, he dis-
proves his analysis as he makes it. He distances himself
from traditional political categories by not understanding
them, and is led to repeat what is older yet. What he offers
as new is a tired romanticism billed as racy. His discussion
of Marcuse and Brown, Marx and Freud, which comes
complete with a fable that reads like an entry to a breakfast
cereal contest, surpasses the "old ideologies" only in by-
passing them.

Roszak illustrates the renewal of banality under the
brand of a new profundity. The key to his thought is the
philistine romanticism that Hegel polemicized against; it
warms up where there is religion, soul, and homilies and
grows cold around thought and analysis. It is not by chance

that Roszak finds Antonioni's *Blow-up* pornographic or Marcuse pedestrian, and waxes eloquent over Paul Goodman, comparing him to Socrates; leaving his appraisal of Goodman aside, where there is thought and intelligence Roszak finds banality and common sense, and where there is banality he finds genius. He unearths with enthusiasm the intellectual division of labor as if it were buried. In this scheme thought is a private preserve for intellectuals, technocrats, and politicians, while poets and dreamers romp in the playground of art, myths, and soul. Just this filing system killed the magic that Roszak wants to remarket. The sundering of a scientific from a poetic truth is the primal mark of the administrative mind.

A dialectical approach is unknown and uncomprehended by Roszak; he prefers the logic of either/or. To follow his crucial political-philosophical discussion for a moment,[18] alienation is either a social or psychic phenomenon. Roszak concludes that "alienation . . . is primarily psychic, not sociological. It is not a propriety distinction that exists *between* men . . . but rather a disease that is rooted *inside* all men. The true students of alienation, therefore, are not social scientists, but the psychiatrists." From this we learn that "The revolution which will free us from alienation must be primarily therapeutic in character." Of course this makes sense, because the establishment would have it no other way, and coincidentally Roszak also has learned "that alienation, properly understood, has been more heavily concentrated in the upper levels of capitalist society than in its long-suffering lower depths."

Not satisfied with this discovery, Roszak goes on: what bothers him is that "alienation" not safely monopolized by literary and psychic repairmen might spill over into soci ology, and suggest that the evil lies not in the human condition but in inhuman conditions. Following Bell's researches on this point,[19] Roszak assures us that alienation in Marx "has only the most marginal connection with the way this idea functions in the thinking of Kierkegaard or Dostoyevsky or Kafka" as if the Big Three on Alienation copyrighted the term for the exclusive use of their dealers and customers. The reified categories that Roszak has made his own paralyze any critique that would undo reification; even his critique of the madness of science, for all its justness, ends up in madness. The romantic critique of capitalism has its truth; but it is to be articulated as a social critique, not departmentalized and fetishized.[20] The magical consciousness, the "wisdom of the sensitive soul" that he champions as a response to a technocratic society is its refuse, not its negation. In accepting the bourgeois form of reason as Reason itself, Roszak does his bit to perpetuate its reign.

The critique of sham novelty and the planned obsolescence of thought cannot in its turn flip the coin and claim that the old texts — be they of Marx or Freud — are as valid as when written and need no interpretation or rethinking. Rather to be pursued is the very relationship between the original thought and the contemporary conditions. The blind choice of one or the other each has its adherents, and has respectively revealed its consequences. Mechanical repetition has proved lethal to a Marxism that was not rethought but only restated; and it has brought bourgeois social theory to the thriving activity of publishing and forgetting. The relationship between the texts of the past and the present society is one of tension. Within Marxism the nature of this tension is a recurring problem, surfacing in discussions on revisionism and orthodoxy.

The Frankfurt School has dubbed the neo-Freudians "revisionists." The term itself cannot be abstracted from the history of Marxism. To those outside a Marxist tradition, the terms revisionism and orthodoxy lack resonance; and even within Marxism the terms have had such a tortured history that their present meaning is in doubt. Historically revisionism in Germany was centered around Eduard Bernstein. To the orthodox it signified a refashioning of Marxism, which in the name of improvement junked its essence as dated: the revision was an incision that cut out the living nerve of Marxism. The neo-Freudians and their successors no doubt willingly accept the designation insofar as they perceive the alternative as that between an authoritarian orthodoxy and creative humanistic revisions. Erich Fromm sees it exactly in these terms; in an essay entitled "Psychoanalysis — Science or Party-Line?" he does not shrink from labeling Freud and the orthodox Freudians "Stalinists" out to "conquer the world." Of course the alternative is then clear: psychoanalysis "must revise, from the standpoint of humanistic and dialectical thinking ... many of his [Freud's] theories conceived in the spirit of nineteenth-century physiological materialism." [21]

But the blank alternatives of orthodoxy and revisionism, or nineteenth-century materialism and twentieth-century humanism, are not to be retained. In question is not dogma versus change, but the *content* of the change; the latter defines orthodoxy or revisionism, not the former. It can hardly be maintained that the orthodox Freudians have simply been content to repeat Freud, fleeing any change as heresy — nor that Freud himself suppressed innovations. "I am defending Groddeck energetically against your respectability," wrote Freud to the clergyman Oskar Pfister. "What would you have said had you been a contemporary of Rabelais?" [22] From Ernest Jones's work on Hamlet and nightmares, to Georg Groddeck's and Sandor Ferenczi's studies, and more recently to Marcuse's *Eros and Civilization* and Norman O. Brown's *Life Against Death*, Freudian concepts are developed and unfolded. Next to these, the revisions, commencing with Adler's, through to Horney's and Fromm's, and sustained by the myth of Freud as authoritarian in theory and person, have been marked by a monotonous discovery of common sense.

Once the false opposition between orthodoxy and revisionism as that between obsolete dogma and contemporary insight is avoided, the notion of orthodoxy must be reformulated. To the point that the theories of Marx and Freud were critiques of bourgeois civilization, orthodoxy entailed loyalty to these critiques; more exactly, *dialectical*

loyalty. Not repetition is called for but articulation and development of concepts; and within Marxism — and to a
degree within psychoanalysis — precisely against an Official Orthodoxy only too happy to freeze concepts into for-
mulas. Revisionism was indeed change, but change that
diluted and dissolved critical insights already gained. It
capitulated to a reality that proclaimed itself as new and
dynamic while statically serving up more of the same. The
outline of the nature of revisionism within both Marxism
and psychoanalysis already emerges: in both forms it is
associated with a decline of theory per se, a refusal or inability to conceptualize. In both forms it edged toward
empiricism, positivism, pragmaticism, and a rejection of
theory — either of the philosophical and Hegelian content
of Marxism or the metatheory of psychoanalysis. In both
forms it sought immediate gains, one in political reforms,
the other in therapy, at the expense of a nonimmediate
theory.

To a great extent the critique of revisionism within
Marxism — at least in the pre-Stalin years — and within
psychoanalysis turned on this point: the revisionists were
accused of suppressing the theory in favor of momentary
gains and reforms. Rosa Luxemburg observed the "hostility
to 'theory' " of the revisionists. "It is quite natural for people
who run after immediate 'practical' results to want to free
themselves from . . . our 'theory.' " [23] In different terms, to
be discussed below, the same is true about psychoanalytic
revisionism. Marcuse found that the tension between theory
and therapy in psychoanalysis, analogous to the tension
between theory and praxis in Marxism, is lost by the revisionists; and in losing this, the revolutionary and critical
edge of psychoanalysis is blunted.

If revisionism is marked by a decline of theory, dialectical orthodoxy reworks and rethinks. In Freudian thought,
however, it is difficult to find a conceptual center that lo-
cates which concepts are worthy of reformulation and
which are inessential. What Georg Lukács did for Marxism
in "What Is Orthodox Marxism?" has not been done for

Freudianism. Yet Freud and his students are clear enough as to what in psychoanalysis is to be preserved — not by thoughtless repetition but by reworking: the concepts of repression, sexuality, unconscious, Oedipal complex, infantile sexuality.[24] It is no accident that two books heretical in their scope and argument but orthodox in their allegiance to the concepts of Freud begin almost identically. "According to Freud," runs the second sentence of Marcuse's *Eros and Civilization*, "the history of man is the history of his repression."[25] And Norman O. Brown's *Life Against Death* begins: "There is one word which, if we only understand it, is the key to Freud's thought. That word is 'repression.'"[26] Brown footnotes this sentence of Freud: "The doctrine of repression is the foundation stone on which the whole structure of psychoanalysis rests, the most essential part of it."

Not to be forgotten — indeed to be explained — is that the push toward immediate reforms and gains, the impatience with past theory, is humanist in motivation. Within psychoanalysis exactly those who sought to make it more liberal and social cut its strength. So far as the post-Freudians make claim to a humanity and sensitivity that they find lacking in psychoanalysis and behaviorism, they are to be taken seriously; open and undisguised apologies for a lethal social order are self-critiques. The promises of liberation, however, are to be scrutinized.

An illustration of this dynamic of humanist reforms versus theory is seen in the Fromm-Marcuse dispute. In 1955 Fromm called Marcuse a nihilist because unlike himself, the humanist, Marcuse did not designate the concrete immediate links and gains that tied the present to the future.[27] To Fromm, Marcuse seemed more committed to theory than practical reforms. The logic of Fromm's argument caused him to cast off (as illogical) the theory that seemed impractical, so as to praise immediate gains and reforms as utopia itself. This becomes evident in a recent work in which in slightly different terms he renews his charge that Marcuse is a nihilist. "Marcuse is not even concerned with politics; for if one is not concerned with steps between the present and the future, one does not deal with politics, radical or otherwise." Fromm adds a bit of psychoanalytic wisdom to explain this situation. "Marcuse is essentially an example of an alienated intellectual who presents his personal despair as a theory of radicalism." [28]

Fromm, on the other hand, unalienated and hopeful, has no difficulty finding the practical "steps." The irony is that the steps that Fromm designates are not only more impractical than anything Marcuse ever discussed, but are steps which even if practiced do less than reform; the loss of theory takes its revenge by confounding the practice that leads deeper into this society with the practice which leaves it. "After a few more years of this *practical policy*," wrote Luxemburg about the reformists, "it is clear that it is least practical of all." [29] "I submit," writes Fromm, "that if people would truly accept the Ten Commandments or the Buddhist Eightfold Path as the effective principle to guide their lives, a dramatic change in our whole culture would take place." If this "dramatic change" seems unlikely or impractical Fromm has some other ideas on how to reach the future more quickly and efficiently. "The first step could be the formation of a National Council which could be called the 'Voice of American Conscience.' I think of a group of, say, fifty Americans whose integrity and capability are unquestioned.... They would deliberate and issue statements which, because of the weight of those who issued them, would be newsworthy." [30] This is only the first step. Fromm explains how Clubs will be formed to help the Council, then Groups, and so on; all of this will alter the nature of society. The advocate of immediate practice, impatient with critical theory, turns into the homespun philosopher promoting the miracle effects of a little elbow grease. The last page of this book, *The Revolution of Hope,* is a tear-out to be sent in with proposed candidates for the National Council of the Voice of American Conscience. The page, however, lacks a prepaid envelope, for as Fromm tells the reader: ."I have not provided a prepaid envelope; the reason follows from what is said in the book. Even the first small step requires initiative at least to address the envelope yourself and spend the money for a stamp." Social change for the cost of a stamp is the wisdom of the humanist denouncing as nihilism the theory exposing the post-card mentality. The revolution of hope is a Walt Disney production. " 'Nihilism,' " wrote Marcuse, "as the indictment of inhuman conditions may be a truly humanist attitude. . . . In this sense I accept Fromm's designation of my position as 'human nihilism.' " [31]

And the new or not-so-new left? It is undoubtedly part of the injustice of this book that it considers as related phenomena nonpolitical psychologies that at best claim to be liberal and humanist, and a political left and the psychology of R. D. Laing and David Cooper that claim to be revolutionary. Certainly they are not equal phenomena. A discussion of Laing and Cooper will be deferred to the final chapter. As for the political left, no matter how confused, it is not to be equated with psychologies serving indifferently big business during the week and employees on the weekends. Yet they are not unrelated. Both have gravitated toward subjectivity — the person and his or her immediate emotions — as a response to a callous and indifferent society. In taking the person as the patient they have followed society's own patent remedy: the individual with a little help from friends can heal the wounds. If the prescription seems double strength with the addition of a sexual ingredient, it is only a variant of an old home medicine.

That American business and its negation — the left — have come to agree on some points as to how to assuage the discontent is an irony that suggests the potency of bourgeois society: there is no escape, not even for those who resist. Society ineluctably coerces everyone to attend to the remaining fragments of self and subjectivity. It is no secret that at least since World War I, and increasingly since the Hawthorne experiment at Western Electric in the

1930s, industrial sociology and psychology have turned to studies of small groups and the subjective condition of the workers.[32] In concentrating on the subjective attitude of the workers and not the conditions of the workers, the intent was to increase production. Hugo Münsterberg wrote in 1913 that scientific management sought to organize work so that "the waste of energy will be avoided and the greatest increase in efficiency of the industrial enterprise will be reached." This is to be done not by "excessive driving of the workingmen . . . on the contrary, the heightening of the individual's joy in the work and of the personal satisfaction in one's total life development belongs among the most important indirect agencies of the new scheme." [33] The official statement of the American Management Association of 1924 noted, "The day when American management can afford to treat the human factor as 'taken for granted' has gone by, and today emphasis must be laid on the human factor in commerce and industry, and we must apply to it the same careful study that has been given during the last few decades to materials and machinery." [34]

Again it is not just to equate developments within American industry with those within the American left; evidently the concern of the latter with the emotional and psychic individual is not directed toward increasing capitalist production, but if anything toward transforming it. Yet it is the very problem that this political goal degenerates more and more into slogans, externally attached, not internally united with the ongoing praxis; the slogans serve to label political groups and factions, not to mark distinct political projects. The ongoing political praxis is diverted into the exploration of the psychic life of the group, sapping of energy sustained political thought and praxis. Politics becomes an afterthought. It is interesting to note, in fact, that the liberal industrial sociologists and human relations experts who pioneered the sensitivity groups and T-groups in the late 1940s and early 1950s — and which parts of the left fantasized that they had invented some 20 years later — were concerned with exactly this development. One of the original purposes of the T-groups was to train participants in human "skills" so they could become effective leaders of social change, particularly racial integration, in their own communities. Yet to the disappointment of some of the originators, even this limited social goal became lost, absorbed by the process of social interaction. The outside and social issues seemed "less involving and fascinating" than the "here-and-now happenings which of necessity focused on personal, interpersonal, and group levels." "Emphasis upon organization and community structures in the back-home situations of members was also greatly reduced." Attention was diverted to "the interpersonal events occurring between trainer and members or between members, and in varying degrees, group events. . . ." [35]

The convergence from contrasting directions on the importance of the subject as an emotional and psychic entity points to a real development of society; not, as the apologists would have it, that society has fulfilled the basic material needs and is moving on to the higher reaches of liberation, but the reverse: domination is reaching the inner depths of men and women. The last preserves of the autonomous individual are under siege. Today human relations are irregulars and seconds at the closing days of the warehouse sale of life. The lines form because everyone knows the rest is junk; all that remains are the remains. In any case talk of satisfaction of the basic material needs is obscene given the world's absolute need and suffering that serve as the means for such satisfaction. Within this context of grim necessity freedom too is grim: the desperate flight from the specter of misery. The smile buttons seek to chase from mind the daily carnage and drudgery; one smiles because the living are sad. The flaunted sensitivity survives only by an iron indifference to the general deprivation and brutalization. The whole program, in brief, is grin and bear it.

The subjectivity that surfaces everywhere, be it in the form of human relations, peak-experiences, and so on, is a response to its demise; because the individual is being administered out of existence — and with it individual experience and emotions — it takes more effort than ever to keep the last fragments alive. Psychic suffocation haunts the reified. The desperation of men and women, for good reason, increases visibly. Today the process of reification is a storm tide; and the human subject is locked in the basement. The frantic search for authenticity, experience, emotions, is the pounding on the ceiling as the water rises.

Within the social and psychological thought that has arisen to explain and respond to these developments, psychoanalysis shows its strength; it demystifies the claims to liberated values, sensitivities, emotions, by tracing them to a repressed psychic, social, and biological dimension. In a period of renewed idealism — talk of ego conflict, moral problems, value conflict — it is unfashionably materialistic; it keeps to the pulse of the psychic underground. As such it is more capable of grasping the intensifying social unreason that the conformist psychologies repress and forget: the barbarism of civilization itself, the barely suppressed misery of the living, the madness that haunts society. Critical theory as critique and negative psychoanalysis resists social amnesia and the conformist ideologies; it is loyal both to an objective notion of truth and to a past which the present still suffers.

II

Revisionism: The Repression of a Theory

> "Let us make no mistake; this day
> and age has rejected me and all I had
> to give."
>
> S. FREUD, 1934 [1]

Alfred Adler was the first to challenge the theories of "the professor," as Sigmund Freud was known to his students. Adler's refashioning of psychoanalysis, which culminated in his break with Freud in 1911, contained all the elements found in the later contributions of the neo- and post-Freudians. Here as later, the new formulations were executed in the name of a more humane, liberal, and social consciousness. Here as later, a shift took place from theory and metatheory to practice and pragmatism, from a sexual and psychic depth and past to a nonsexual psychic surface and present. Here as later, subjectivity, in the guise of the "individual," was added to psychoanalysis. Adler later dubbed his psychology "individual psychology." "Individual Psychology tries to see individual lives as a whole . . . [It] is of necessity oriented in a practical sense." [2]

Freud's critique of Adler lay the groundwork for the critical theory critique of the neo-Freudians. Both these critiques suggest the weakness of the post-Freudians: liberal revisions traded the revolutionary core of psychoanalysis for common sense. Psychoanalytic revisionism as worked out by Adler was already associated with a retreat to pleasantries and homilies. Freud's link to a Hegelian tradition

19

— with which he otherwise shares little — is in the deliberate renunciation of common sense. "A person who professes to believe in commonsense psychology," Freud is reported saying once, "and who thinks psychoanalysis is 'far-fetched' can certainly have no understanding of it, for it is common sense which produces all the ills we have to cure." [3]

Orthodox psychoanalysis is orientated in the reverse direction: toward uncommon sense, exactly the farfetched. "The truth of psychoanalysis lies in its loyalty to its most provocative hypotheses." [4] "In psychoanalysis only exaggeration is true." [5] Adler and those who have followed him have labored to escape the uncommon concepts of repression, infantile sexuality, and libido since they "run counter to the prejudices of convention." [6] Freud has ascribed Adler's popularity exactly to his flair for the ordinary: he has created a theory which is in tune with common sense, which "recognizes no complications, which introduces no new concepts that are hard to grasp, which knows nothing of the unconscious, which gets rid at a single blow of the universally oppressive problem of sexuality." [7] Freud was well aware of the conformist and conservative bent of Adler's revisions. He observed that the additions to or revisions of psychoanalysis contain "what is already known from other sources or what can be most easily related to it. Thus . . . what is selected . . . with Adler [is] egoistic motives. What is left over, however, and rejected as false is precisely what is new in psychoanalysis and peculiar to it . . . the *revolutionary and embarrassing advances of psychoanalysis.*" [8]

The irony that it was exactly socialists and liberals who cut out the "revolutionary and embarrassing advances" of psychoanalysis is the irony of the encounter of psychoanalysis with social and socialist thought. Freud himself, in discussing Adler's break with psychoanalysis, remarked on the importance of the "socialist element" in Adler. [9] Ernest Jones also offered as an explanation for the Adlerian shift away from the repressed consciousness to the sociological consciousness the fact that the Adlerians were socialists.[10] Yet it was exactly this shift that dulled the critical and social powers of psychoanalysis. From the beginning the repression of psychoanalysis was announced as its liberalization.

The young Adler considered himself a socialist; his first book, in 1898, on the occupational and health hazards of the tailor trade has been called a "synthesis of socialism and medicine." [11] According to a biography by a friend, Adler was among a group of students who studied Marx, though he was not influenced by the economic theories of Marxism; rather he studied the "sociological conception on which Marxism is based." [12] Another account states that Adler was well acquainted with Marxist literature.[13] In any case it seems to have fallen to Adler to have written the first paper explicitly on Marx and psychoanalysis, "On the Psychology of Marxism." This was delivered in Freud's Vienna Society in 1909 but, never published, seems to be lost. It is preserved in some form by Otto Rank's notes of the session. According to the notes, Adler showed that an "affective state" — sensitivity — underlies class consciousness. "Because this affective state always seeks to fend off degradation, it is impossible for the class conscious proletariat to adopt an attitude of fatalistic resignation. . . . In conclusion Adler wishes to stress that Marx's entire work culminates in the demand to make history *consciously.*" [14]

The drift of Adler's concern, here as elsewhere, was essentially confined to a *conscious* dimension: first organ inferiority-compensation, degradation-sensitivity, and, later, inferiority-masculine protest. In the Vienna Society, shortly following this presentation, Adler would make explicit his critique of Freud, and would leave the Freud circle. Freudian notions of repression and libido, sexuality and infantile formation made way for inferiority and its compensation, a nonsexual desire to rule or be above. Adler questioned whether the "driving force" in neurosis was Freudian repression or an "irritated psyche," [15] and responded by indicating the importance of "adjustment" and education. "Educational influences which smooth the way for the child are of far-reaching significance here. . . . If one intervenes early with intelligent tactics, a condition results which might be described as one of carefree cheerfulness. . . . Mistakes in education, on the other hand . . . lead to such frequent disadvantages and feelings of displeasure that the child seeks safeguards." [16]

The liberal and practical bent of Adler's writing and thought is evident. Many of his early essays are concerned with correct education, proper upbringing, and so forth. "The need for affection becomes the lever of education. A hug, a kiss, a friendly look, a loving word can only be obtained when the child subordinates himself to the educator via the detour of culture." "A great many educational applications follow from this." [17] It is not surprising that socialists interested in educational reform were drawn to Adler. Alice Rühle-Gerstel, the wife of Otto Rühle, an anti-Stalinist communist, wrote in *Freud und Adler* that insofar as Adler sought to make men cooperative "he worked in his Individual Psychology as a democratic influence and as a cultural preparer for socialism." [18]

Adler's early critiques of Freud removed any doubt about his fundamental break with psychoanalysis. In *The Neurotic Constitution* (1912) he claimed that three of Freud's "fundamental views" were erroneous. The first was that the "libido is the motive force" behind neurosis; rather it was a "neurotic goal." The second and third were the notion of the sexual etiology of neurosis and the importance of infantile wishes. For Adler these "infantile wishes already stand under the compulsion of the imaginary goal." Neurosis develops out of "the feeling of uncertainty and inferiority and demands insistently a guiding, assuring, and tranquilizing position of a goal." [19]

Later critiques by Adler would add little. In "The Difference between Individual Psychology and Psychoanalysis" (1931), Adler wrote that Freud forgot the "wholeness of the personality" "which [concept] represents the essential contribution of Individual Psychology to modern

medicine. . . . This wholeness penetrates every psychological part-phenomenon and colors it individually. . . ." The
Freudian notion of an essential antagonism between the
individual and a repressive society, between pleasure and
reality, is dismissed; rather, society is in fact the best
friend of the individual, who is innately inferior and uncertain. "Social interest is the compensatory factor for the
physical inferiority feeling of man. . . . We can regard society as the most important compensatory factor for human
weakness." [20] The Adlerians, in the name of "individual
psychology," take the side of society against the individual.
One Adlerian accuses Freud of advancing the notion of
"Society the Oppressor"; to this Adlerian what must be
faulted is not society's "hostile frustration" of the neurotic,
but the neurotic's "failure to adapt to society." [21]

The distance that Adler traveled from psychoanalysis
can be found in nearly any passage of his writings from
the 1930s. Depth analysis makes way for moral rearma-
ment; neurotics and psychotics are themselves guilty of
forsaking the benefits of a guiltless society. "All failures,"
wrote Adler, listing "neurotics, psychotics, criminals,
drunkards, problem children, suicides, perverts and pros-
titutes," are "failures because they are lacking in fellow
feeling and social interest. They approach the problems of
occupation, friendship and sex without the confidence
that they can be solved by cooperation." [22] Or to take a
more specific analysis: narcissism signifies a "lack of social
interest" and "self-confidence." The person "has not learned
to do justice to the tasks with which he is confronted." [23]

The substance of the response of Freud to Adler pre-
figured the response of the Frankfurt School to the neo-
Freudians. Both objected to the substitution of everyday
wisdom for the advances of psychoanalysis: the replacement of an instinctual dynamic by social factors or interest,
repression and sexuality by insecurity and goals, depth
psychology by surface psychology. For Freud and critical
theory, to the point that sexuality, repression, libido are revised out of psychoanalysis, psychoanalysis is itself re-

pressed. "Instead of analyzing sublimation," wrote Adorno of the neo-Freudians, "the revisionists sublimated the analysis itself." [24] The inner dynamic of individual and society is severed and replaced by a mechanical model of the individual adjusting or maladjusting to values, norms, goals, and so on. These "values" and "norms" are not examined as the coin of a repressive society, but are traded and exchanged at face value.

In the discussions in the Vienna Society that preceded the break with Adler in 1911, Freud denounced the revisions. "The whole doctrine has a reactionary and retrograde character." Instead of delving into the unconscious, Adler sticks to "surface phenomena, i.e. ego psychology," and succumbs to the ego's own misconceptions. The ego's denial of its own unconscious is transmuted into a theory. Freud designated two objectionable features of Adler's work: an antisexual and a reductionist trend. The first denies the sexual basis for neuroses, while the latter ignores individual and distinct forms of psychic phenomenon; rather it asserts the "sameness of all neuroses," deriving them all from the identical wish for superiority. These were more than minor differences. Wilhelm Stekel's comment that Adler's contribution was merely a "deepening and extension" of psychoanalysis was rejected out of hand by Freud. "When Stekel maintains he finds no contradiction between these ideas and Freudian theory, I want to point to the fact that two of the participants do find a contradiction, namely Adler and Freud." [25]

In *The History of the Psychoanalytic Movement* Freud further elaborated his objections to Adler. Adler presented a theory which was compatible and familiar to the ego. He adopted the viewpoint of the ego instead of uncovering the ego's own foundation. Freud did not simply reject "ego psychology" — and this becomes important later — but argued that psychoanalysis was unique precisely in passing beyond the ego and exposing what was previously taboo: sexuality, unconscious, libido. Adler takes the "opposite view" and stays exclusively on the surface. From the beginning, Freud claimed, Adler never evinced "any understanding of repression." Rather he surrendered to the "jealous narrowness of the ego" which was unwilling to acknowledge its own unconscious.[26] In the *New Introductory Lectures* Freud restated some of these objections: no matter what the case is, the Adlerians will declare that the motive is the wish to overcome inferiority. While there is "*something* correct" in this "a small particle is taken for the whole."[27]

Adler's later thought succumbs to the worst of his earlier banalization. It is conventional, practical, and moralistic. "Our science . . . is based on common sense. . . ." Common sense, the half-truths of a deceitful society, is honored as the honest truths of a frank world. "The insane never speak in the language of common sense which represents the height of social interest. . . . If we contrast the judgment of common sense with private judgment, we shall find that the judgment of common sense is usually nearly right."[28] He wrote in another book, "The purpose of the book is to point out how the mistaken behavior of the individual affects the harmony of our social and communal life; further, to teach the individual to recognize his own mistakes, and finally to show him how he may effect a harmonious adjustment to the communal life."[29]

That it was the socialist Adler and later liberal neo-Freudians who rendered the psychoanalysis of Freud apologetic and conformist formulates the problem. In brief, the political content and impact of the work of Adler and the neo-Freudians were determined by the psychological and sociological concepts they employed, *not* by their manifest political attitudes. Similarly, Freud's subversiveness is derived from his concepts and not from his stated political opinions. This disjunction is absolutely crucial to recognize: the disjunction between the political, social, and truth content of concepts and the political-social outlook of those using the concepts. They are not identical; they often stand in contradiction. The apparent mystery of Marxists defending the theory of the conservative Freud against openly liberal Adler and his successors is founded on this disjunction. Critical theory clings to the radical concepts of psychoanalysis, exactly what Adler and his followers weakened.

If Freud was "conservative" in his immediate disregard of society, his concepts are radical in their pursuit of society where it allegedly does not exist: in the privacy of the individual. Freud undid the primal bourgeois distinction between private and public, the individual and society; he unearthed the objective roots of the private subject — its social content. Freud exposed the lie that subject was inviolate; he showed that at every point it was violated. The neo- and post-Freudians, enthusiastic as they were for the individual or person, did not dig into these categories; rather they were spellbound by their surfaces.

No matter how heretical the neo- and post-Freudians imagined they were in theorizing about the "values," "insecurities," "goals," of the individual, they were safely following the official ideology of the private and autonomous individual and consumer. It is the context and content of these concepts that dictate the retrograde political meaning of their psychology. The psychoanalytic concepts of Freud, even against himself, trespassed on psychic private property; to the forces of conformity Freud is guilty of breaking and entering the private psychic household. Even if Freud in the end justifies civilization, he has in the interim said enough about its antagonistic and repressive essence to put it in question. The reverse is true of the revisionists: whatever criticisms of society they advance are absolved by the concepts and formulations that point toward health and harmony.

It should be recalled that in any case Freud was not simply a reactionary. Notably, his essay " 'Civilized' Sexual Morality and Modern Nervousness" is a plea for changes in sexual morality, a plea to be found in many of his other writings. "We have found it impossible to give our support to conventional sexual morality or to approve highly of the means by which society attempts to arrange the practical problems of sexuality in life. We can demonstrate with ease that what the world calls its code of morals demands more sacrifices than it is worth." [30] Or one can find statements such as this, a favorite of left Freudians: "It goes without saying that a civilization which leaves so large a number of its participants unsatisfied and drives them into revolt neither has nor deserves the prospect of a lasting existence." [31]

Similarly, one can overstate the socialism and liberalism of the Adlerians. It seems that Adler himself, at least by the later 1920s, quickly shed what there was of his socialist past and affinities. Moreover, according to one left Adlerian, Adler in his later years became a bitter opponent of the leftists among his adherents; he charged them with compromising his teachings, and he did everything possible to undermine them.[32] This seems to be reflected in the writings of Adlerians, which in general show no more, and often less, overt left political sympathies than those of the Freudians. As remarked above, they facilely defend society against the individual — hardly a liberal position. The interest in society is transformed into a defense of society. From this perspective Freud is feared as the radical he actually is. "The attack on religion," writes one Adlerian, "must also be seen as part of Freud's larger attack upon ethical standards and social interest generally." [33]

Yet the loyalties of Freud himself lay with modified repression, even if his concepts did not. Critical theory thinks through these concepts; it values Freud as a non-ideological thinker and theoretician of contradictions — contradictions which his successors sought to escape and mask. In this he was a "classic" bourgeois thinker, while the revisionists were "classic" ideologues. "The greatness of Freud," wrote Adorno, "consists in that, like all great bourgeois thinkers, he left standing undissolved such con-

tradictions and disdained the assertion of pretended harmony where the thing itself is contradictory. He revealed
the antagonistic character of the social reality." [34]

The characterization of Freud as a great bourgeois
thinker illuminates the Marxist criteria for evaluating non-
revolutionary thinkers. A parallel can be established between Marx's judgment on Ricardo and the post-Ricardians
and critical theory's appraisal of Freud and the post-
Freudians. To Marx, Ricardo was the classic and best
representative of bourgeois economics since he articulated
the contradictions of bourgeois society without glossing
them over. He was "scientifically honest" because unlike
Malthus he did not seek to "accommodate" his science to
outside "alien, external interests." [35] Those who came after
Ricardo sought to reconcile what Ricardo left antagonistic. Hence, James Mill sought to systematize Ricardo,
that is, to harmonize and neutralize him. "What he tries
to achieve," wrote Marx, "is formal, logical consistency.
The *disintegration* of the Ricardian school 'therefore' begins with him. With the master what is new and significant
develops vigorously amid the 'manure' of contradictions
out of the contradictory phenomena. . . . It is different
with the disciple. His raw material is no longer reality, but
the new theoretical form in which the master has sublimated it." The disciple seeks "to *explain away* reality." [36]

The necessity to synchronize the contradictions, in
turn, is derived from a shift in the historical conditions
which makes these contradictions more threatening; "scientific" opinion is increasingly faced with the choice of
turning decisively critical or openly apologetic. Marx noted
about two post-Ricardian economists, Bastiat and Carey,
that they understood that socialism and communism were
theoretically founded in classical political economy, which
had openly expressed the contradictions of society. "Both
of them therefore find it necessary to attack, as a misunderstanding, the theoretical expression which bourgeois
economy has achieved historically in modern economics,
and to demonstrate the harmony of the relations of produc-

tion at points where classical economists naively designated this antagonism." [37]

The business of harmonizing the unpleasant contradictions of Freud was the joint task of Adler and the neo-Freudians. The issue is not the direct influence of Adler on the neo-Freudians, though that does not seem to be lacking, but a parallel effort: the logic and reasoning of their argument. The close relationship has been noted by many. Adler's loyal editor, Heinz L. Ansbacher, cites several textbooks indicating the affinity. "It has to be said that Adler's influence is much greater than is usually admitted. The entire neo-psychoanalytic school, including Horney, Fromm, and Sullivan, is no less neo-Adlerian than it is neo-Freudian. Adler's concepts of sociability, self-assertion, self, and creativeness permeated the theories of the neo-analysts." [38] An article in an Adlerian journal, "Karen Horney and Erich Fromm in Relation to Alfred Adler" argues the same point. [39] Clara Thompson, herself a neo-Freudian, also established the parallels: that "man seeks to solve his problems by the search for the way to feel superior" was "an important discovery" of Adler. "It has much in common with Horney's 'Idealized Image' and Sullivan's idea that maintaining an inadequate self-system is a potential source for increasing anxiety." Further, Horney "revised with new emphasis Adler's idea of the importance of the patient's neurotic goals." In Horney, as in Adler, the patient is sick not because of past events, but because in coping with past events he or she established poor goals and "false values." [40]

The critique of Freud that the neo-Freudians advanced concentrated on his nineteenth-century materialism that was allegedly impervious to individual and social factors. To correct this, they, like Adler, added social values and goals, notions of self and self-image; these additions were to take into account a relationship between the individual and society which Freud had omitted. Critical theory reverses this appraisal; Freud's "biologism," his apparent disregard of social values, is his strength. It constitutes the critique of bourgeois individualism; Freud's materialism peels back and away the social "norms" and "values" to find the inner social dynamic. It is necessary, wrote Max Horkheimer, to follow Freud's biological materialism, "to stick to Freudian orthodoxy in this fundamental sense." [41]

Exactly what has been called the contribution of Adler and the neo-Freudians, the discovery of self or personality,[42] is the loss of the critique of the individual. The Freudian concepts exposed the fraud of the existence of the "individual." To be absolutely clear here: the Freudian concepts exposed the fraud, not so as to perpetrate it, but undo it. That is, unlike the mechanical behaviorists, the point was not to prove that the individual was an illusion; rather it was to show to what extent the individual did not yet exist. To critical theory, psychoanalysis demonstrates the degree to which the individual is de-individualized by society. It uncovers the compulsions and regressions that maim and mutilate the individual. From this perspective the formulations of the revisionists are already concessions to liberal ideology.

When the revisionists do confront the ailment of the individual they imagine it can be healed by mere invocation. Instead of dissecting the self to search for the internal and social injury, they appeal to its goodness and wholeness. Freud's analysis moves on another plane. Freud undermines, wrote Marcuse, "one of the strongest ideological fortifications of modern culture — namely, the notion of the autonomous individual." "His psychology does not focus on the concrete and complete personality as it exists in its private and public environment, because this existence conceals rather than reveals the essence and nature of the personality." Rather he dissolves the personality and "bares the sub-individual and pre-individual factors which (largely unconscious to the ego) actually *make* the individual: it reveals the power of the universal in and over the individuals." [43] "Personality," wrote Freud, "... is a loosely defined term from surface psychology that does nothing in particular to increase understanding of the real processes, that is to say, *meta-psychologically* it says nothing. But it is easy to believe that one is saying something meaningful in using it." [44]

The "sub-individual and pre-individual factors" that define the individual belong to the realm of the archaic and biological; but it is not a question of pure nature. Rather it is *second nature*: history that has hardened into nature. The distinction between nature and second nature if unfamiliar to most social thought is vital to critical theory. What is second nature to the individual is accumulated and sedimented history. It is history so long unliberated — history so long monotonously oppressive — that it congeals. Second nature is not simply nature or history, but frozen history that surfaces as nature. [45]

Unlike the revisionists Marcuse holds to Freud's quasibiological concepts, but more faithfully than Freud himself — and against Freud, unfolds them. The revisionists introduce history, a social dynamic, into psychoanalysis from, as it were, the *outside* — by social values, norms, goals. Marcuse finds the history *inside* the concepts. He interprets Freud's "biologism" as second-nature, petrified history. The chapter in *Eros and Civilization* "The Historical Limits of the Reality Principle" is a historical reading of Freud's concepts. Marcuse attempts to show that the "repressive organization of the instincts" is "due to *exogenous* factors — exogenous in the sense that they are not inherent in the 'nature' of the instincts but emerge from the specific historical conditions under which the instincts develop." [46]

This is no arbitrary construct tacked onto Freud. Rather Freud himself in his metatheory — exactly what the neo-Freudians reject — derived the instinctual biology from a prehistory of violence and force. This is where Freud comes closest to Nietzsche: civilization is a scar tissue from a past of violence and destruction. This is the authentic materialistic and historical core of Freud's thought. "In the last resort it may be said that every internal compulsion which has been of service in the development of human beings was originally, that is, in the evolution of the human race nothing but an external one," wrote Freud in a small essay "Thoughts for the Times on War and Death." [47] In an extract from a letter that Jones prints this is stated even more succinctly. Responding to an inquiry by Jones on the "true historical source of repression," he wrote, "every *internal* barrier of repression is the historical result of an *external* obstruction. Thus: the opposition is incorporated within [*Verinnerlichung der Widerstände*]; the history of mankind is deposited in the present-day inborn tendencies to repression." [48] The whole of Marcuse's historical reading of Freud is contained in these sentences.

For Freud the "higher" civilized "values" are grounded in "lower" ones. Social right is condensed social violence. "Right is the might of a community. It is still violence, ready to be directed against any individual who resists it. . . . The only real difference lies in the fact that what prevails is no longer the violence of an individual, but that of a community." [49] Internalized in the individual, values derive both from the archaic conflict of the sons against the father and from the reenactment of the Oedipal conflict. The superego is founded on guilt rooted in the failure of the uprising against the father-oppressor. "It must be said that the revenge of the deposed and re-instated father has been very cruel; it culminated in the dominance of authority." "The dead now become stronger than the living had been, even as we observe it today in the destinies of men. What the father's presence had formerly prevented they themselves now prohibited in the psychic situation of 'subsequent obedience.' " [50] Or in the less provocative language of *The Ego and the Id*: "We can give an answer to all those whose moral sense has been shocked and who have complained that there must surely be a higher nature in man. 'Very true,' we can say, 'and here we have that higher nature, in this ego ideal or super-ego, the representative of our relation to our parents. When we were little children we knew these higher natures, we admired them and feared them; and later we took them into ourselves." [51]

As Freud himself knew this was the cutting and revolutionary edge of psychoanalysis: the refusal to accept social and individual values abstracted from the concrete struggle of men and women against themselves and nature. Here critical theory follows Freud; he is revolutionary in that his theory is critical and materialistic. Psychoanalysis pulls the shrouds off the ideology of values, norms, and ethics which is the stuff of Adler and the post-Freudians. For this very reason Freud considered the efforts of Ludwig Binswanger to add values to psychoanalysis "conservative." [52] The values that the neo- and post-Freudians esteem are pieces of history scrubbed clean of their carnal and visceral origins. They prize them because they have forgotten their corporal origins. Marcuse is correct: "Fromm revives all the time-honored values of idealistic ethics as if nobody had ever demonstrated their conformist and repressive features." [53]

The twentieth-century modernizers confidently leave Freud behind as a bad memory from the nineteenth century. Yet as Adorno has remarked, it is the revisionists and modernizers who witlessly reproduce nineteenth-century theories. In their insistence on the role of values, morals, and milieu, they have upheld a dated, mechanical and pre-Freudian schema. There is nothing new or novel about the idea of the individual as an autonomous monad which is affected by outer forces.

> While they [the revisionists] unceasingly talk of the influence of society on the individual, they forget that not only the individual, but the category of individuality is a product of society. Instead of first extracting the individual from the social process so as then to describe the influence

which forms it, an analytic social psychology is to reveal
in the innermost mechanism of the individual the decisive
social forces.[54]

The revisionists, rather, posit the individual as an independent unity which is influenced from without. In
bestowing on the individual autonomy and values, the
neo-Freudians accumulate ideology. The critical path lies
elsewhere; it entails burrowing into the individual and independent subject; it means penetrating the categories of
individual and society, not merely juggling them. The
individual, before it can determine itself, is determined by
the relations in which it is enmeshed. "It is a fellow-being
before it is a being." [55]

To shift terms for a moment: critical theory pursues the
dialectic of the particular and the universal. Following
Hegel, it finds the whole is the truth; that is, the particular
is formed and informed by this whole: society. To discover
society within the psyche of the individual — the universal
within the particular — is to discover the objective nature
of the prevailing subjectivity; it is to strip away the floss of
the autonomous individual. Exactly this was the program
of psychoanalysis; it revealed the sway of the universal —
society — within and over the individual. Psychoanalysis,
wrote Horkheimer, "discovers the historical dynamics of
society in the microcosm of the monad, as it were, in the
mental conflicts of the individual." [56] Psychoanalysis, wrote
Marcuse, "elucidates the universal in the individual experience. To that extent, and only to that extent, can
psychoanalysis break the reification in which human relations are petrified." [57]

This was unacceptable to the neo-Freudians. The relation of the particular and the universal, the individual
and society, was not presented as one of mutual mediation;
rather they presupposed a simple model of individual-
society interaction that operated on the surface. If their
formulations on the individual-society relation seem only

slightly different from those of critical theory, the *political* meaning of the difference can be discerned in the Fromm-Marcuse dispute. Both claim the dialectical construction. In this exchange, the nature and social consequences of the "productive" "happy" individual that Fromm prescribed were at issue. Marcuse, in his critique of the neo-Freudians and Fromm, posed an either/or. Marcuse wrote "Either one defines 'personality' and 'individuality' in terms of their possibilities *within* the established form of civilization, in which case their realization is for the vast majority tantamount to successful adjustment. Or one defines them in terms of transcending content." This would "imply transgression beyond the established form of civilization, to radically new modes of 'personality' and 'individuality' incompatible with the prevailing ones.... This would mean 'curing' the patient to become a rebel." [58] To Fromm these words are proof that Marcuse forgot "his own dialectical position to the extent of drawing a black and white picture." Rather there are "important qualifications" to make. The "qualifications" are that there are exceptions. "I agree with Marcuse that contemporary capitalist society is one of alienation." "But I disagree entirely with the view that as a consequence these qualities [of happiness and individuality] exist in nobody." Though, to be sure, they are "rare." [59]

Yet to the extent that one addressed oneself to the exceptions, as exceptions, to that extent the social whole is repressed and forgotten. The alleged exceptions redefine and reformulate the totality of the whole society: they restrict and delimit it. The inner and depth dynamic of the individual-society relation is forsaken for a take-it-or-leave-it attitude; with skill and effort a destructive society can be safely ignored. Marcuse notes that the neo-Freudian distinctions between good and bad, constructive and destructive, productive and unproductive are "not derived from any theoretical principle, but simply taken from the prevalent ideology.... The distinction is ... tantamount to the conformist slogan 'accentuate the positive.' Freud was right; life is bad, repressive, destructive — but it isn't *so* bad, repressive, destructive. There are also constructive, productive aspects. Society is not only this, but also that." Left out is how "under the impact of civilization the two 'aspects' are interrelated in the instinctual dynamic itself, and how the one inevitably turns into the other by virtue of this dynamic." [60] The point is not that "love and happiness" are mere ideology. Crucial, wrote Marcuse in a rejoinder to Fromm's response, is the "context" in which they are defined and proclaimed. "They are defined by Fromm in terms of positive thinking which leaves the negative where it is — predominant over the human existence." [61]

If the difference between the two positions seems like a minor philosophical quarrel, the result is not. The year following *Eros and Civilization* (1955) and this exchange, Fromm published *The Art of Loving*, a book that suggests the distance separating the neo-Freudians from critical theory. Fromm opens on the same note made in his rejoinder to Marcuse; he acknowledges the negative power of society and advises that the "art" of loving is rare. "In a culture in which these qualities are rare, the attainment of the capacity to love must remain a rare achievement." Only on the last four pages does "an important question" arise: "How can one act within the framework of existing society and at the same time practice love?" Footnoting Marcuse, Fromm repeats his argument: "One must admit that 'capitalism' is in itself a complex and constantly changing structure which still permits a good deal of nonconformity and of personal latitude." However "people capable of love under the present system are necessarily the exceptions." [62]

The either/or that Fromm objected to in Marcuse is found in his own thought. In Marcuse it is defined by the political and social whole; its meaning derives from its place within the social contradictions — an either/or of complying or resisting society. With the neo-Freudians it is shifted to the individual, personal, and psychological which are only loosely in contact with society. The exceptions that Fromm discovers and promotes are the exceptions that liberal society has always flaunted as proof of its essential beneficence; with a little effort at home anyone can be spared a deadly and loveless world. Love and happiness are repairs for the do-it-yourselfer. Yet to critical theory these exceptions are confirmations of the very brutality and injustice they ideologically leave behind. Sensitivity and warmth for the few, and coldness and brutality for the rest, is one of the stock notions and realities that feed the ongoing system. Love within a structure of hate and violence decays or survives only as resistance. The neo-Freudians escape the social contradictions that sink into the very bowels of the individual by repressing them.

A half-truth is contained in the neo-Freudian revisions, as there is in all revisionism: the notion that reality is historical, and theory, if it is to be adequate to that reality, must also be historical and must also change. This returns to the problem of orthodoxy and revisionism; again what is in question in defining these terms within both Marxism and Freudianism is not change per se, but the *quality* or *content* of change. There is no repudiation of change within psychoanalysis, but it is change that remains loyal to the content of the original concepts. This dialectical loyalty demands both fidelity to the critical edge of the concepts and allegiance to a historical reality.

To critical theory, psychoanalytic concepts undergo change in direct relation to their object: the individual. Psychoanalysis as a theory is embedded in the same historical dynamic that created as well as mutilated the individual. Adorno's statement that the "prebourgeois order does not yet know psychology, the oversocialized one knows it no longer," [63] is incomprehensible if psychoanalysis is abstracted from the fate of the individual. Psychoanalysis as a science of the individual survives exactly as

long as the individual survives; it is historically situated
where the individual is situated. It was unknown where
the individual was yet to emerge as a semiprivate being,
and it is becoming unknown and forgotten in the "post"
bourgeois order where the individual is superfluous. The
story of the rise, fall, and forgetting of the individual is
the tale of the rise, fall, and repression of psychoanalysis.
"Some of the basic assumptions of Freudian theory ...
have become obsolescent to the degree to which their object, namely the 'individual' as the embodiment of id, ego,
and super-ego has become obsolescent in the social reality." [64]

The individual of "classic" psychoanalysis managed
to eke an existence out of the relatively underdeveloped
market; this was the truth in the early bourgeois theories of
the free individual and the free and competitive market
— a truth, that is, which was confined to the middle
classes. For the proletariat the notion of the free individual
was always a sham. With the centralization and synchronization of the market, the individual lost its relatively independent and private sources of sustenance. Fi-
nance capital, unlike liberalism, "abhors the anarchy of
competition and seeks organization." [65] It wants direct
domination. The individual that had subsisted in the recesses and corners of the market is eliminated by organized capital. "Under monopoly capitalism the individual
has only the chance of a short reprieve." [66]

As the early forms of competition pass into direct
control and manipulation, the individual exits. "The social
power structure," Adorno wrote, "hardly needs the mediating agencies of the ego and individuality any more." [67]
Mediation turns into immediate command and suggestion; the very notion of individual psychology becomes
problematic. "In a thoroughly reified society, in which
virtually no immediate contacts exist between men and
in which every man ... is reduced to a mere function of the
collective, the psychological processes, although they per-

sist in the individual, no longer appear as decisive forces of the social process." The psychology of the individual, according to Adorno, has lost its emphatic meaning and substance.[68]

Yet "That which is obsolete is not, by this token, false." [69] Insofar as the psychoanalytic concepts are wedded to a "classic" capitalist model, they can throw into relief the subsequent historical evolution of a psychic and extra-psychic reality: the erosion and corrosion of the individual and the immediate context of the individual, the family. These are decisive secondary changes of the transformation from "free" to monopoly capital. The family is one of the crucial terms. Social changes are refracted through the family and in turn affect the formation of the individual. The "mental" household of the individual is constructed out of the family household; as the latter shrinks to an efficiency unit, so does the former.

The single most important fact in the transformation of the family is the decay of the economic significance of the father as the relatively independent provider and power. As the father loses the remnants of independent authority and individuality, the family loses its resiliency. If there are positive and democratic features of this process, there are also negative ones; the child ego once nurtured and scarred by the family is no longer nurtured but simply integrated.

> The actual weakness of the father within society, which in-
> dicates the shrinkage of competition and free enterprise,
> extends into the innermost cells of the psychic household;
> the child can no longer identify with the father, no longer
> can accomplish that internalization of the familial demands,
> which with all their repressive moments still contributed de-
> cisively to the formation of the autonomous individual.
> Therefore there is today actually no longer the conflict be-
> tween the powerful family and the no less powerful ego;
> instead the two, equally weak, are split apart.[70]

Critical and psychoanalytic theory cannot be indifferent to such developments — developments which here can only be stated not demonstrated. The concepts of ego and superego are themselves affected by the restructuring of the family. The reformulating of the concepts, in particular to account for the ego, has in fact characterized much of psychoanalytic and neopsychoanalytic literature for the past thirty years. It is hardly accidental that ego psychology — psychology that predominantly explores the ego — emerges just when the ego as an autonomous unit turns openly suspect.

Yet the particular readings and interpretations of the ego diverge widely. Ego psychology of the psychoanalytic revisionists took up the ego as a welcome relief from Freud's excessive attention to the id and unconscious; like the rest of their program it promised to neutralize Freud's materialism and biologism. Furthermore this ego psychology fit in well with the newer psychologies of self, self-image, and so on. Critical theory reverses this approach; the ego is studied not as an advance over or repression of psychoanalysis, but as an inner development of psychoanalysis. Attention to the ego does not demand blindness toward the instinctual and social dimensions that constrict and choke the ego.

Where one dates the emergence of ego psychology depends on one's loyalties. The Adlerians would date it from Adler — "the father of ego psychology" [71] — and draw direct and indirect links to the later developments of psychoanalysis and the neo-Freudians. "The first pioneering steps toward ego psychology within psychoanalysis were taken by Alfred Adler." [72] The Freudians, of course, are anxious to deny this origin, and usually date ego psychology from Freud's own later works, e.g., *The Ego and the Id* (1923), or from works by Freudians, especially Anna Freud's *The Ego and the Mechanism of Defence* (1937), Heinz Hartmann's *Ego Psychology and the Problem of Adaption* (1939), and Herman Nunberg's "Ego Strength and Ego Weakness" (1939). As Hartmann maintained from the first, referring to the Adlerians, "Psycho-analytic ego psychology differs radically from 'surface psychologies.' " [73]

Yet substantively, if not factually, the Adlerians may be correct; the prevailing ego psychology, even in its psychoanalytic form, does not differ essentially from surface psychology. For this reason it is Adlerian (and pre-Freudian) in its lack of interest in the libido and the unconscious. Briefly, Heinz Hartmann — probably the most important of the Freudian ego psychologists — detached the ego, or part of the ego, from the unconscious and libidinal drives; he dubbed this the "conflict-free ego sphere." "Not every adaption to the environment, or every learning and maturation process, is conflict." The critical edge of Freud is blunted: the aim of psychoanalytic therapy is "to help men achieve a better functioning synthesis and relation to the environment." [74] As Adorno wrote of Anna Freud's book, it evinces "the reduction of psychoanalysis to a conformist interpretation of the reality principle." [75] In ego psychology the same expurgation of psychoanalysis takes place as with the neo-Freudians, who themselves draw upon psychoanalytic ego psychology. As with Adler, the "socializing" of psychoanalysis, in seeking to account for the reality of society, drains psychoanalysis of its blood. With Hartmann, even if he is alert to the dangers of sociologism, tho "indwelling tendency" of his concepts, to follow a recent critique, is one of "reduction." [76]

Those who laud these theoretical developments within and outside psychoanalysis have told the unpleasant truth pleasantly. Ego psychology grinds down the cutting edge of psychoanalysis; it refashions the outlandish quality of psychoanalysis in contemporary garb. "Just as *conflict* is the central notion in Freud's work, *adaption* is central in Hartmann's. . . . Compared to Freud, Heinz Hartmann is another breed altogether; not a revolutionary, but a practical earth-bound traditionalist." [77] Another sympathizer candidly admits, "There was a radicalism, even a shocking quality, to many of the early psychoanalytic formulations;

contemporary ego psychology has a tamer, more 'healthy-minded' quality." [78] Or in a similar vein it has been noted that "without the revisions which the neo- and post-Freudians have brought to psychoanalysis, one may doubt whether it could have been as attractive to middle-class Americans." [79] Finally, one theorist who draws the links between psychoanalytic ego psychology, the neo-Freudians, and the post-Freudians, sums up the contribution of what he calls ego psychology's " 'great departure' from classical doctrine." With Freud, the scope of the ego was "minimized" and was held in "low esteem." But "ego psychology . . . paves the way for a positive appreciation of the human ego." This is joined with the "rediscovery and the rehabilitation of the old-fashioned idea of the self" by the neo-Freudians. [80]

Critical theory does not join the general approbation. The "positive appreciation" of the ego is the song and dance of social amnesia; it forgets the pain by whistling in the dark. What is crucial, however, is not to ignore the study of the ego, but to denounce the presupposition that the study of the ego is inseparable from its praise. While undeniably there was a shift in the later Freud toward the ego, this was a shift that occurred within a psychoanalytic framework. The unconscious, libido, and so on, were not surrendered; rather they were explored within the ego itself. Freud did, in *The Problem of Anxiety* (1926), dissociate himself from those psychoanalysts who, following his earlier work, made into a *Weltanschauung* the theory of "weakness of the ego in relation to the id." While Freud eschewed all *Weltanschauung*, several pages later one can find a statement that seems unrepentant. "The act of repression has demonstrated to us the strength of the ego, but it also bears witness at the same time to the ego's impotence and to the uninfluenceable character of the individual instinctual impulse in the id." [81]

Adorno has remarked that the defect of neo-Freudian and positivist thought is that it is unable to comprehend the ego as simultaneously a psychic and an extrapsychic phenomenon — the ego as dialectical. Within a positivist consciousness, attention to ego psychology proceeded only at the cost of id psychology. It remained imprisoned in the either/or logic. Freud sought to retain both moments and, moreover, foresaw clearly that a turn to ego psychology would entail a renunciation of the specific gains of psychoanalysis. Ego psychology formed the prehistory of psychoanalysis; hence ego psychology *within* psychoanalysis must "have a different look" from nonpsychoanalytical ego psychology.[82] A letter of Freud to Jung in 1909 is a testament to Freud's insight, showing him keenly aware of the dangers of an either/or mentality, and of the threat — in Adler and Jung — of ego abstracted from depth psychology.

> We have already agreed that the basic mechanism of neurosogenesis is the antagonism between the instinctual drives— the ego as the repressing [force], the libido as the repressed. ... It is remarkable though, that we human beings find it so difficult to focus attention equally on both of these opposing drives.... Thus far I have really described only the repressed, which is the novel, the unknown, as Cato did when he sided with *causa victa*. I hope I have not forgotten that there also exists a *victrix*. Here Adler's psychology invariably sees only the repressing agency, and therefore describes the "sensitivity," this attitude of the ego toward the libido, as the basic cause of neuroses. Now I find you on the same path . . . that is because I have not sufficiently studied the ego, you are running the risk of not doing justice to the libido which I have evaluated.[83]

Critical theory is loyal to both dimensions. It accepts and studies psychoanalytic notions of the "weak" ego; this, however, is situated in a social dynamic that turns into an instinctual one.[84] A repressive society drives the ego to regression and unconsciousness so as to irrationally subsist. Critical consciousness and the autonomous ego, inextricably linked, dissolve under the impact of a massified society.

Marcuse uses a term of Franz Alexander's, "corporealization of the psyche," to suggest the psychic process: the translation of psychic energy into "unconscious automatic reactions." "The reality principle asserts itself through a shrinking of the conscious ego in a significant direction: the autonomous development of the instincts is frozen, and their pattern is fixed at the childhood level." [85]

The psychoanalytic concept of narcissism captures the reality of the bourgeois individual; it expresses the private regression of the ego into the id under the sway of public domination. Adorno considers it one of Freud's "most magnificent discoveries." [86] It is no accident, according to Adorno, that Freud turned to ego psychology and narcissism in such works as *Group Psychology and the Analysis of the Ego;* that is, in direct reference to mass and social phenomena.[87] The drive of this small work — which is one of the most cited by the Frankfurt School — is to show the inseparable relationship between the individual and mass psychology. "From the very first individual psychology . . . is at the same time social psychology as well." [88]

Narcissism comprehends the dialectical isolation of the bourgeois individual — dialectical in that the isolation that damns the individual to scrape along in a private world derives from a public and social one. The energy that is directed toward oneself, rather than toward others, is rooted in society, not organically in the individual. "Narcissism means in psychoanalysis: libidinally cathecting of one's own ego instead of the love for other men. The mechanism of this shift is not the least the society that puts a premium on the hardening of each individual — the naked will to self-preservation." [89] Narcissism is the stuff not only of the irrational mass movement but of the irrationality of everyday life, because it is unconscious. The ego regresses, making "its supreme sacrifice, that of consciousness." [90]

If the history of psychology is the history of forgetting, Adler was the first, but by no means the last, to forget. His revision of psychoanalysis was a homemade remedy to assuage the pain of the unfamiliar: psychoanalysis. The notions that he, and the neo-Freudians, would champion were borrowings from everyday prattle: the self, values, norms, insecurities, and the like. They were offered as antidotes to Freud's illiberalism. Yet just this constituted Freud's strength: his refusal to bow to reigning wisdom; his exploration of a tabooed and erotic psychic underground that officially did not exist. The subjectivity and social factors the revisionists added to correct Freud's excesses did the trick; they brought psychology back into the fold.

III

Conformist Psychology

The neo-Freudian shift from a psychology of the unconscious to one of the conscious, from id to ego, sexuality to
morality, repression to personality development, and most
generally from libido and depth psychology to surface and
cultural psychology, accelerated with the post-Freudians.
The neo-Freudians had done their work well; their successors no longer needed to respond to Freud. Psychoanalysis is too remote, too impersonal, too intellectual, too
materialistic. The past is honored and forgotten. To replace it, neo-Freudian revisions are revised once again.
Stripped of Freudian remnants they arrive in an existential
package: themes of the real self, personality, actualization.
"Authenticity," the password of a synthetic society, smooths
the way.

The core of the post-Freudian contribution is subjectivity.
The subterranean explorations of Freud cast doubt on the
autonomous subject; they revealed an individual shot
through with sedimented layers of history — reminders
and remains of a psychic, carnal, and erotic conflict of
men against men, men against civilization. The claim that
the individual was a private preserve was exploded. The
response of the neo-Freudians, and of the post-Freudians
who follow their lead, is to shore up common sense: to
assuage any suspicion that the individual is not master of
the house. With the post-Freudians the subject is affirmed
and confirmed. Where psychoanalysis delves and dissects,
the former accepts and combines; where psychoanalysis
is negative, the former is inspirational.

Neither the content nor the popularity of the post-

Freudians can be abstracted from the social and cultural environment. Their work suggests liberation now — without the sweat and grime of social change. They promise to unleash or tap the real self and real emotions: the authentic individual. From their perspective, the very move from a Freudian biological and instinctual psychology toward a humanist, existential, and personal one is proof of how far industrial society has progressed toward liberation: we are now ready for the final freedom — the subjective and psychological individual.

Yet this may be exactly wrong. A different interpretation is possible: subjectivity is disintegrating under the impact of a massified society. The ego — or self, individuality, subjectivity — moves to the fore in psychological thought just as in fact it is preparing to exit from existence. This is hardly an accidental development; because the ego's existence is challenged, attention is focused on it. There is talk of identity and identity crises, security and insecurity, authenticity and bad faith, not because there is a viable ego faced with too many options, but because there is no ego faced with no options. The revisionists misread this even as they correctly read it as the prevailing quest for security. As with much of their analysis, this is true but superficial; hence false. This particular misreading throws into relief the distinction between Freud's alleged biologism and the cultural accent of the neo- and post-Freudians; it becomes evident that Freud's biologism is concentrated history while the historical consciousness of the post-Freudians is dressed-up biology. For the revisionists take what is a product of history and society — anxiety and insecurity — and translate it into a universal element of man's being — into biology. They gain existentialism and lose history. Fromm wrote that "Life, in its mental and spiritual aspects, is by necessity insecure and uncertain." *"Free man is by necessity insecure."* [1]

Within psychoanalytic theory, anxiety and insecurity are not universalized but are read as the price that a repressive civilization exacts from the individual. Observing

the prevalence of "inner resolution and craving for authority," Freud stated that one of its principal causes was "the
impoverishment of the ego due to the tremendous effort
in repression demanded of every individual by culture."[2]
The orientation of the theory is clear: personal insecurity
is a direct response to collective repression. It is not a universal component of man's essence. In other terms: repression is not obsolete; rather it assumes a new form which
is manifested by the threatened ego's quest for security.
To be secure in one's property and person is one of the
oldest bourgeois war cries; the cry is reheard when one's
psychic person is endangered. The social forces are squeezing out the individual as an inefficient unit. The cost of
securing and expanding advanced capital is private insecurity. Engels once wrote that although organized labor is
able in a certain measure to retard the growth of misery
"what certainly grows is the uncertainty of existence."[3]
The existence of insecurity is due to the insecurity of
existence·

This is registered in, but is not comprehended by, the
popular ego psychology of the neo- and post-Freudians.
They mirror, not penetrate, surface phenomena. The drive
for security is accepted as such, and is not traced to an
insecure existence within the insecure collectivity. As with
Adler, secondary and primary things are confused. In the
confusion the negative is lost; "personality" and "identity,"
"becoming" and "authenticity" move to the fore as unad-
vertised specials of the affluent society which already is a
bargain hunter's delight. "When material needs are largely
satisfied," writes Carl Rogers, "as they tend to be for many
people in this affluent society, individuals are turning to
the psychological world, groping for a greater degree of
authenticity and fulfillment."[4] The clear distinction between material and psychic needs is already the mystification; it capitulates to the ideology of the affluent society
which affirms the material structure is sound, conceding
only that some psychic and spiritual values might be lacking. Exactly this distinction sets up "authenticity" and

"fulfillment" as so many more commodities for the shopper. Rather it is the fissure itself which is the source of the ills — between work and "free" time, material structure and psychological "world," producers and consumers. Rogers accepts the fissure and prescribes a double dose as the cure: after a hard day on the job, the weary are to unwind with a little "authenticity." This is the same message forced in through every pore by the media; the attention of the discontented is diverted from the source to the surface. One is to suppose that the emptiness of life is due more to the reruns on television than to the runaround itself. Against Freud's nineteenth-century provincialism one is offered twentieth-century ideology.

Ideology is the content and form of Allport's *Becoming*, published the same year, 1955, as *Eros and Civilization*. If the latter strives to articulate the contradictions of the social reality, the former seeks to silence them. The latter speaks of repression, the former of becoming. There is little suggestion that today to become is to succumb, to capitulate. Allport talks another language, one scraped clean of negativity. It only affirms and confirms. Hints, still found in the neo-Freudians, of sickness and neurosis, sexuality and repression, civilization and its discontents, are unacknowledged and unknown. The sublimation that sexuality underwent with the neo-Freudians is the starting place for more. The result is a text befitting the high-school graduation speeches it has undoubtedly inspired. "Happiness is the glow that attends the integration of the person while pursuing or contemplating the attainment of goals." The consciousness or the superego, derived by Freud from the power and violence of the father and society, and rooted in the dread of group exorcism, is banalized to a "value-related obligation," a "wholly positive and immediate sense of obligation, of self-consistency." [5]

Lingering thoughts of neurosis and sickness, doubts about the price and toll of civilized repression, are admitted only to be waved aside as thoughts for and of the sick. A report reaches Allport "that after the turmoil of painful symptoms subsides, many patients still ask the question 'What do I live for?' But these distressing cases, however frequent, merely underscore their departure from the human norm." The "human norm" is unthinkingly upheld as if it were truth itself, not the coagulated terror and misery of individual and social history. If Freud examines the neurotic and the sick, Allport sticks to the normal and the cheerful. The sick must be avoided, for their very existence puts into question what is not to be questioned: the rationality of the whole. Allport inches close to the basic bourgeois notion that linked the unemployed vagabonds and the mad as twin violators of virtue and sanity.[6] He writes, alluding to Freud, that some theories of "becoming" "are based largely upon the behavior of sick and anxious people. . . . Fewer theories have derived from the study of healthy human beings. . . . Thus we find today many studies of criminals, few of law-abiders, many of fear, few of courage, more on hostility than on affiliation; much on blindness in man, little on his vision."

The positive and inspirational note is not accidental. As Marcuse observes, the neo-Freudians read like Sunday sermons. So do the post-Freudians. The positive is promoted so as to drive out the negative. One strives to be cheery because it is a cheerless world. Since reflection on the latter is taboo, Allport, like others, seeks to make palatable the unswallowable: the lie that the isolated and abandoned individual can "become," "love," "be." Hence, the "how to" nature of their works; in this they follow Fromm, who denies the self-help sell even as he affirms it. In *The Art of Loving* he tells us not to expect "easy instructions in the art of loving." One finds, however, instructions; the rub, apparently, is that to love one needs a "total personality;" it is off-limits for the alienated. With that established one can begin. "If we want to learn how to love we must proceed in the same way we have to proceed if we want to learn any other art, say, music, painting, carpentry, or the art of medicine or engineering." As with carpentry, there are four prerequisites: discipline, concentration, patience, and supreme concern.[7] Unlike carpentry, however, in loving one should avoid "bad company" whose "orbit is poisonous and depressing." Rollo May in *Man's Search for Himself* accepts the designation of a self-help book. No cheap and instant cures are proffered, we are told, but in a "worthy and profound sense every good book is a self-help book — it helps the reader ... gain new light on his own problems of personal integration." [8]

One helps oneself because collective help is inadmissible; in rejecting the realm of social and political praxis, individual helplessness is redoubled and soothes itself through self-help, hobbies, and how-to manuals. It is an old formula to keep bourgeois society on its tracks: while business dominates mind and body, one is admonished to mind one's own business. "Rebellion acts as a substitute for the more difficult processes of struggling through to one's own autonomy, to new beliefs," writes Rollo May, as if one could struggle through to one's own autonomy without rebelling. The eclipse of freedom by economic oligarchies is not necessary, Rollo May tells us; they "need not destroy freedom if we keep our perspective." Now we have time for "*inward* psychological and spiritual freedom." The "perspective" that guarantees freedom — inward freedom — is the first gimmick of the apologist. An unjust reality is spiritualized away; with some persistence, everyone is or can be free. The full litany of virtues that the rich once preached to the poor are restored to service. Inward courage, discipline, strength, humility are proffered by these homespun philosophers as a patent medicine for a lethal civilization. "The question of which age we live in is irrelevant," writes May in an age of genocide and technological bombing. "No traumatic world situation can rob the individual of the privilege of making the final decision with regard to himself, even if it is only to affirm his own fate," he tells us, as if affirming one's own death, and not life itself, were the essence of freedom.[9]

An existential impulse is common to many of the post-

Freudians. May, Allport, Maslow, and Rogers all con-
tributed to a small volume entitled *Existential Psychology*.
It is, however, an existentialism thoroughly cleansed and
sterilized of its European accents, so as to be fit for home
consumption; its grating edges have been ground down in
the name of a happy-go-lucky American ethos. Whatever
truth there is to the clichés that European existentialism
was spurred by the deathcamps and resistance to fascism,
and hence is tinged with pessimism and gloom, is too
much truth for its American representatives: they want an
existentialism that poses no threats to their optimism and
good cheer. European existentialism, we are told by Allport, is too "preoccupied with dread, anguish, despair
and 'nausea.'" American existentialism is "more optimistic." Or writes May, the "tragic aspects" of existentialism
do not mean it is pessimistic. "Quite the contrary." Or
Maslow informs us that "we need not take too seriously
the European existentialists' harping on dread, on anguish,
on despair, and the like." [10]

We need not take it seriously for within the American
scene the negative turns into a positive, an added attraction for the already popular main event. Tragedy, alone-
ness, death, render life more "profound." Maslow talks of
the tragic sense of life as if it were the special flavor of the
month; it is to spark an otherwise dull selection. It adds a
"dimension of seriousness and profundity of living" which
is to be "contrasted with the shallow and superficial life."
A pinch of death is prescribed as the antidote to the dull
life. If, as Adorno has remarked, Heidegger transforms the
fact of death into a professional secret for academics, the
existential psychologists tell the secret to a public that has
already heard the news. They promote dying as if it were
going out of business.

The formula that Maslow follows is an old one: add soul
to misery and injustice and they turn soulful and virtuous.
The designation of "deep," "profound," "authentic," as
applied to existence, meaning, art, which recurs throughout

the writings of the post-Freudians follows the worst of a romantic tradition. The inability to conceptualize, to articulate the content of existence or art, makes way for glorification and edification. The reified mind is awed to thoughtless respect before the mere fact of culture — as if it were automatically profound. Hegel, undoubtedly unread by these existentialists, dubbed it "empty depth." "Even as there is an empty breadth, there is also an empty depth . . . an intensity void of content — pure force without any spread — which is identical with superficiality." [11] Or as he wrote elsewhere, "What possesses a deep *meaning*, means absolutely nothing." [12]

All of this is believed to constitute progress in psychological thought. The neo-Freudians balked at Freud's interest in sexuality and the psychic past; in their place, they put moral and cultural problems of the adult. "Neurosis, itself," wrote Fromm, "is, in the last analysis, a symptom of moral failure." [13] The post-Freudians take off from there as if they were pioneers of the back country exploring a well-policed suburbia. "One's *present* philosophy of life may hold the key to one's conduct," writes Allport. Discoveries that "patriotism" or "stamp collecting" could be "*ultimate* needs" — and not sexual desire — are presented as if they were the long-suppressed truth, and not, as they are, long oppressive common sense.[14] The regression to a pre-Freudian position, where one knows nothing of the unconscious, repression, and sexuality, but only of surface motives, interests, and desires is claimed to be a great advance. This confusion bestows on the discoverers of banality the air of courage and adventure: they defend the status quo as if it were the revolution. They creep toward the line of the reactionary which has it that it takes nerve to defend the establishment nowadays, and it is conformist to attack it.

In reality, until the reified society dissolves, it is the reverse. So too with intellectual disciplines, such as sociology and psychology. One attacks Marxism as if one's career might well be wrecked, and not secured by it. Or psychoanalysis is presented as if it were state policy, thus implying its critics are rebels. Similarly, the continual use of the first person in the writings of post-Freudians suggests that they are putting themselves on the line, when in fact they are toeing it. Aside from some gentle jabs at crude behaviorism, little characterizes this existentialism better than its intellectual obsequiousness. To read a collection such as Allport's *Personality and Social Encounter* is to find the banalities of the age set forth as exciting research projects for the future. Colleagues, friends, acquaintances are continually commended for naming things already named, discovering things already discovered, suggesting things everyone knows. Continual thanks is offered to "philosophers," "sociologists," "theologians," as homogeneous groups, for reminders, suggestions, contributions; assumed is a harmonious universe where contradictions have melted into good-natured friendships between departments monotonously restating the same point.

The project of deepening Freud by appending values, meaning, and morality to a psychic and carnal reality is one of diluting by adding. Profundity is supposedly gained by relocating the misery of life from the material to the spiritual. Such a tactic, Adorno wrote, runs the risk of the culture critic who, bemoaning the breakdown of "values," ascribes the problem "to the advanced state of the human spirit rather than the retarded state of society." [15] The world is too materialistic, we are told, and we need some spiritual values to patch things up. The patching bespeaks the usefulness of the spiritual values supposedly beyond the infamy of the material world. Abstracted from the realm of truth they once inhabited, they are promoted for what they can do, not what they are. Religion, divested of truth, turns synthetic and pragmatic. Rollo May tells us religion is useful as "it strengthens the person in his sense of his own dignity and worth, aids him in his confidence." The spiritual values bear the imprint of the nonspiritual market: exchange value. Nothing is for itself, everything is for something else. Pragmatism reigns supreme. Religion and philosophy degenerate to a radio format: early morning pitches to sustain one through a joyless day. The superficial critique of a spiritless reality, by confusing bad materialism with too much materialism, mollifies the discontented into taking more of the same.

A passage from Viktor Frankl's *Psychotherapy and Existentialism* illustrates the existentialist's sham deepening of Freud and psychoanalysis. He wants to add to Freud's "depth psychology" of the instincts and the unconscious a "height psychology" that does "justice to man's higher aspects and aspirations. . . . Freud was enough of a genius to be aware of the limitations of his system, such as when he confessed to Ludwig Binswanger that he had 'always confined' himself 'to the ground floor and basement of the edifice.' " [16] Here as elsewhere those who come after the "genius" update and improve him. Yet Freud's remarks to Binswanger are not as Frankl presented them; they are the opposite. Freud knew well enough and criticized often enough the tendency — especially among the Swiss such as Pfister, Binswanger, Jung — to sublimate psychoanalysis into religion and morality by ignoring its psychic and erotic base; this was the approved way of making his "limited" system more acceptable. It was no welcome addition; and further in his remarks to Binswanger, which Frankl omits and thereby distorts, Freud observed the political meaning of such revisions and sublimations. He wrote to Binswanger

> You have failed to convince me. I have always confined myself to the ground floor and basement of the edifice — You maintain that by changing one's point of view, one can also see an upper story in which dwell such distinguished guests as religion, art, etc. You are not the only one to say this; most cultured specimens of *homo natura* think the same thing. In this you are conservative, and I revolutionary.[17]

Another passage from Allport crystallizes the mode as well as the content of a central post-Freudian revision. In an essay from 1953 which advances the novel idea "that the best way to discover what a person is trying to do is to *ask* him," Allport states, "I am fully aware of the heterodoxy in suggesting that there is, in a restricted sense, a discontinuity between normal and abnormal motivation, and that we need a theory that will recognize this fact." [18] The first person formulation, Allport's full awareness of the heresy, suggest a risk that is nowhere to be found; he alludes to the courage of the heretic while colluding with the authorities. His heterodoxy is to defend the established church. Everyday wisdom has it that the healthy and the mad belong in — and should be put in — different worlds. One of Freud's greatest contributions was his insistence on the reverse, that normal and abnormal, healthy and sick formed a continuum. Differences were merely quantitative, but not qualitative. As he said in his American lectures, "Let me at this point state the principal finding to which we have been led by the psychoanalytic investigations of neurotics. The neuroses have no special psychic content that is peculiar to them and that might not equally be found in healthy people." [19]

Here as elsewhere the effort of the neo-Freudians and post-Freudians has been to shunt aside the unpleasantness of Freudian theory; where Freud insists on the bond between the healthy and sick, they opt for the good news that keeps them separate. Maslow's entire psychology is oriented toward the healthy and toward saving them from contamination by the ill. He prefers "a direct study of good, rather than bad human beings, of healthy rather than sick people." The world of suffering and misery, of the damaged and maimed, melts away. Maslow's remembering to remind indicates how much he has forgotten. "We should be careful to note that the tendency to grow toward full-humanness and health is not the *only* tendency to be found in the human being." [20]

The fetish of health, success, adjustment finds expression in the case histories presented. Freud's cases concerned the sexually unfree, with deep anxiety and phobias.

The existentialists, rather, turn to presidents, administrators, astronauts to tell us about the secrets of existence. Maslow inspires us with the achievements of Olympic gold-medal winners.[21] Allport is fond of the story of the man whose "dominant passion" was to be a polar explorer; his success in this presents the "issue squarely" — how a "central commitment" enables one to withstand other temptations. Elsewhere, in telling us how a "healthy adult" develops an active value schema which in turn "exerts a dynamic influence upon specific choices" he cites the case of a Harvard president. The formula for his mode of operation — that of the "overworked administrator" — is that "each specific issue fits readily into one of a few dominant categories (schemata) of value. If the administrator is clear in his own mind concerning his value orientation . . . decisions on specific issues automatically follow." [22] So a tale of value-integration. A standard technological and bureaucratic mode of classification is presented as the latest contribution to humanity. Viktor Frankl, connoisseur of meaning and existence, sums it up; psychology, the effort to fathom the psyche of the autonomous individual, here passes into its negation: open ideology for the forces and powers that render the autonomous individual and psyche irrelevant. He quotes a "height psychologist" to the effect that what is needed is a "basis of convictions and beliefs so strong that they lifted individuals clear out of themselves and caused them to live and die for some aim nobler and better than themselves." He adds, "And who is this height psychologist that I have just quoted? The speaker was not a logotherapist, nor a psychotherapist, a psychiatrist, or a psychologist, but the astronaut Lt. Col. John H. Glenn, Jr." [23]

The words leave little to add: this psychology is the ideology of conformism and synchronization in the era of late capitalism. The reality of violence and destruction, of psychically and physically damaged people, is not merely glossed over, but buried beneath the lingo of self, meaning, authenticity, personality. The more these cease to exist, the more they are invoked. Personality, suspect in its heyday, is hawked as just the thing for a life already too much a thing. The concepts are less than critical; they are blank checks that endorse the prevailing malpractices with cheery advice on inner strength and self-actualization. Maslow's "peak experience" is the misery of everyday life condensed. Liberation is a banal existence plus enthusiasm. He says as much. "My retrospective impression is that the most fully human people, a good deal of the time, live what we could call an ordinary life — shopping, eating, being polite, going to the dentist, thinking of money, meditating profoundly over a choice between black shoes or brown shoes, going to silly movies, reading ephemeral literature." [24] There can be no doubts here. The ordinary is extraordinary because it is ordinary. The alchemists of liberation transmute the base wares of capitalism into the treasures of humanity.

The post-Freudians are philosophical autodidacts in an age when obsolete autodidacticism is officially perpetuated. A sympathetic appraisal of their writings can only conclude that they have fallen victim to the ravages of the intellectual division of labor which condemns the intellectual voyageur to provincialism. As eagerly as they welcome the philosophy of existentialism, they know little of social theory or philosophy. For this reason, they turn out to be the enthusiastic exponents of the prevailing ideology even as they intend to oppose it. Because they are unacquainted with the theory, philosophy, or history of positivism, their critique of behaviorism — ultimately their *raison d'être* — does not resist behaviorism but complements it. They add soul and values to the facts, thereby fantasizing that the facts themselves change. The naive critique of a value-free factual science issues into a naive celebration of American "values," themselves the products of these facts. Misconceiving the essence of positivism, they conceive the alternative as a renamed more-of-the-same. Unable to escape the dilemmas of nondialectical, nontheoretical thought, they are forced to choose between bad materialism and bad idealism. The prevailing divisions in the intellectual turf condemn them to witless weeding of measured yards.

Their failure is not theirs alone. The decline of philosophy takes place also within philosophy proper. The professional philosopher in keen competition with the natural scientist resolves to be more certain about less. As Freud himself said of approaches which fetishize methodology and ignore content in the name of certainty, "These critics who limit their studies to methodological investigations remind me of people who are always polishing their glasses instead of putting them on and seeing with them." [25] The result is that others, "nonprofessional" philosophers, pick up the discards — values, existence — and handle them as fragile chunks of pure philosophy that would be damaged by analysis. In both cases, within and outside philosophy, the social and political content that defines and informs the concepts drops off. The irrelevancy of the technical philosophical expert generates a response that desperately wants the reverse: to be relevant. Especially in North American psychology, both options are especially crude: mechanistic behaviorism and vapid existentialism. Neither are adequate to an antagonistic reality that turns half-truths into non-truths.

It is impossible here to do more than suggest a critique of positive thought. The difficulty is compounded by the prevailing reified consciousness. The victory of positive thought is so total that the fundamentals of dialectical thought are not so much rejected as not considered. Hence it is nonsense, if not a scandal, to suggest the precepts of a critical theory, i.e., what is immediate as sense perception is not concrete but abstract; or the alternative: the concrete is gained by mediation, by working through the immediate, not accepting it. Yet such notions lie close to the life nerve of dialectical thought, which explains that what is tossed up to view and touch can be viewed and touched, but itself depends on a political and social universe which is not immediately here or now. The facts are conditioned by the factors — society as a whole. To fasten on the facts while forgetting the social content is to fall prey to a mystifying immediacy. In an antagonistic society, appearance and essence, immediacy and mediacy, diverge; things are not what they seem to be. The whole is the truth and the whole is false. Dialectical logic is loyal to the contradictions, not by the reasoning of "on the one hand and on the other," but by tracing the contradictions to their fractured source.

Positivism exists in more than one form. To be aware of these forms is to become aware of their internal connection — and to be wary of alternatives that offer the same while promising relief. The existential psychologists in reacting to behaviorism implicitly or explicitly identify positivism as a repressive scientific discipline which leaves out the human element; and so it does. The positivism of this sort is one part of a complex story. Within Germany, positivism expressed itself differently, and predated in name and fact the positivism that is more associated with Saint-Simon and Comte. A positive theory of law and history was developed that emphasized, against abstract and formal thought, the living and concrete individuality, uniqueness, and particularity of phenomena that defied classification; this positivism sought to defend the particular and the concrete against the general and the abstract.[26]

This form of positivism — which is generally neglected in studies and critiques of positivism — as well as the quasi-natural scientific positivism were subjected to criticism by Hegel and Marx. If the neonatural-science type formulated general scientific laws which deliberately ignored the particular and the individual, the "concrete" positivism defended the existing individualities against abstract thought. The inner connection between these positivisms was an explicitly conservative orientation toward preserving and defending the existing reality; with Saint-Simon and Comte it was directed against the "negativity" of the French Revolution. As Comte wrote, the task of positivism was to "imbue the people with the feeling that . . . no political change is of real importance." [27] The German form — also to be found in Burke — differed in mode; the positive was identified with the organic, with that which grew naturally out of the existing reality: individuality, particularity, local customs and laws. As Marx wrote, to it *"everything that exists is an authority."* [28] The point is that the German positivism is no less a positivism than the French variety and in its form and content is akin to the existential psychological variety.

The irony is that Maslow's efforts in the direction of what he even calls "positive psychology," dealing with "fully functioning and healthy human beings" and not "sick ones," is well within the alternatives offered by positivism itself. The jargon of personality, values, becoming, being, health, is no escape from mechanical behaviorism but its reverse side. Even the French positivism, it should be noted, from Saint-Simon through to Durkheim, possessed an emphatic moral and religious element that was to complete its fetish of the facts. [29] The "positive" of these positivisms is characterized not so much by a definite form as by a definite content; the inner connection between a positivism of numbers and quantities and one of human values and qualities is the excision of a critical distance and theory. Both surrender to different faces of reality — its facts or its ideology — and both stay clear and clean of antagonisms and contradictions.

Existentialism in its philosophical and psychological form, like concrete positivism, sought an immediacy that avoided the abstractions of concepts and mechanical models. Rollo May contrasts a psychology of forces, drives, and reflexes with one of being. Existential psychology, he tells us, centers "upon the *existing* person; it is the emphasis on the human being as he is *emerging, becoming.*" The terms employed — existence, being, man, authenticity — promise concreteness. Yet to critical theory this very concreteness is gained by abstraction. Concepts such as "being" or "existence" possess the flavor of concreteness, not its substance. As Adorno has written in his critique of German existentialism, *Jargon der Eigentlichkeit* (*Jargon of Authenticity*), such concepts reflect reality rather than comprehend it; they are the reified transcendence of reification. The concept of human existence, for example, if compared to the concept of class existence may seem more concrete and immediate and universal; but class existence may be more concrete, not in the immediate, but in indicating the social process that shapes human existence into its prevailing configuration: inhuman for some and human for others. The concept of "human existence" suggests an abstract human condition; "class existence" indicts bad conditions. The former suggests a nonexistent egalitarianism, as if master and slave, owner and worker, bomber and bombed all participate in the same universal abstraction. The conditions, however, are very different and are derived from the social and political whole. The human condition for the rich is the inhuman one for the impoverished. The neat subsumption of an unjust society under concepts such as "existence" and "being" is abstract: it does violence to a concrete reality that is unequally violent.

Existentialism tilts over into ideology, empty moralizing on the being of man. Its egalitarianism exists today only in the negative. For just this reason Marcuse attacked the existentialism of Jean-Paul Sartre; it presupposes a fraudulent equality in which there is no difference between classes and categories of people. Everyone is reduced to an "abstract denominator of a universal essence." What lurks behind this existentialism is the "ideology of free competition, free initiative, and equal opportunity. Everybody can 'transcend' his situation, carry out his own project: everybody has his absolutely free choice. However adverse the conditions man must 'take it' and make compulsion his self-realization." [30] The existential concepts are pseudoconcrete; they parasitically live off the surface of reality while killing the concrete mediations that are decisive: the social process that determines that all are not equally free and unfree, equal neither to "be" nor "become." One talks of "man" when there are psychically and physically maimed men and women. The jargon seduces the theory which is seeking to comprehend the conditions that perpetrate the damage; in shifting the attention from inhuman conditions to "man himself" it seconds these conditions. Hence Adorno's remark, "Der Mensch ist die Ideologie der Entmenschlichung." "Man is the ideology of dehumanization." [31]

Existentialism in its American psychological form barely knows its theoretical sources. For that reason the weakness of European philosophical existentialism is only redoubled by the post-Freudians. With barely a glance toward objective reality, a blinkered and constricted view of "self," "becoming," "authenticity" is promoted. That to be or to become, in a society whose being is one of mass administration and blatant violence, is hardly acknowledged as a problem. What must be acknowledged, for example the prevalence of anxiety, is grafted onto man's essence as if it grew there. Such is the tried and tested method of the apologist: what is social in origin is presented as natural and human. Maslow does not shy away from recommending a little "grief and pain" for "growth and self-fulfillment" as if their short supply would stunt the individual. Humanist psychology turns into its opposite; blind to pain it recommends more as a cure for too much.

Existentialism is bourgeois ideology in the hour of its retreat; because it is no longer able to pierce the mystifications, it settles on the subject, the self. The more the surface of reality deflects attention, the more the deflected focus on the individual. One seeks to compensate for the damages of an external reality by internal scrutiny; the hope is to fan some warmth out of the dead embers as protection against the chill of the outside. It does not work. The subject abstracted from the social context decays into a thing — the very ill existentialism was to cure. What Adorno writes of a tendency of psychoanalysis is true for existential psychology. "The more strictly the psychological realm is conceived as an autonomous, self-enclosed play of forces, the more completely the subject is drained of his subjectivity. The objectless subject that is thrown back on himself freezes into an object." [32]

The fetish of facts by one school of positivism is countered by the fetish of subjectivity by another. The more the development of late capitalism renders obsolete or at least suspect the real possibilities of self, self-fulfillment, and actualization, the more they are emphasized as if they could spring to life through an act of will alone. Hence the naiveté that clings to a name such as "Center for Studies of the Person" with which Carl Rogers is identified, as if "the Person" existed in a no-man's-land of free-floating interpersonal relations, and not in a society that threatens to reify the last spontaneous movements. The modern individual is in the process of disintegration. To forget this is to abet the process not aid the resistance. The existential stress on free and autonomous actions and decisions is a reflex response to a society that is eliminating them. Even French existentialism, for all its despair, Adorno has remarked, is too optimistic. [33] The existentialists bank on an individual solution to the general bankruptcy.

The philosophical naiveté of the post-Freudians is thrown into relief by a question that must be broached, although it cannot be fully developed: the problematic nature of humanism. The existential psychologists and post-Freudians on occasion call their psychology humanistic; at least, the stress on man for himself, man the measure, existing man, expresses the humanist drift of their thought. The progressive note that would unite anyone from Marx to Maslow need hardly be emphasized. Against doctrines that presented reality as given by nature or God, and so located it beyond human change, humanism maintained the relevancy and centrality of man, that is, men *and* women, as actors and creators. The sentence from the early Marx is often cited: to be radical is to go to the root of things, and at the root is man himself. On this level, among

Marx, the existentialists, and liberals, there is little disagreement.

Fundamental differences arise, however, among all these "humanists." In brief, what is in question is mediation. The route from the world of things back to the human source — the subject — is not, as it were, a straight line. If the social reality is ultimately derived from individuals, it is not immediately; rather, it has a drift, a momentum, a weight of its own. For that reason, social reality has "laws" of development that are not identical with the "laws" of the individual psyche. In the face of misunderstanding both within and without Marxism, one must be absolutely clear here; the laws of social development are *not* identical with the laws in the natural sciences. The content of the social laws is not nature but *second nature*: coagulated history.[34] They are manmade, but they also make men; they are dialectical, at once subject and object, neither totally one or the other.

Within Marxism, humanism is dialectical; it testifies to the objectivity of social reality without fetishizing it or ignoring human subjectivity — ultimately human labor — which is its source. Liberal thought — as well as some forms of Marxism — tends to fetishize one or the other moment: to present social reality as utterly independent from man or directly and immediately under his rule. The danger of the latter, more important in the context here, is that it lapses into pure subjectivity. Social reality divested of its objectivity is psychologized away. Psychologism, to follow Adorno, "falls under the sway of contingency and becomes untrue."[35] In reducing everything to the subject and denying the objective truth it loses the ability to distinguish between delusions and realities. Psychologism is the constitutional failing of psychology, psychoanalysis included. Social process and conflicts are read as psychological and individual ones. Society is conceived as simply an individual or psychological pact between men, not as a piece of reality with its own social gravity.

The credo of the humanist is *reductio ad hominem*.

In the eagerness to find humanity, it is seen everywhere, forgetting and so perpetrating the social manufacture of inhumanity. Because everything is immediately human, one need only be a bit more human to cure the evil. This attitude, presented as part of the opposition, is in fact part of the prevailing *Zeitgeist*. A paradigm could be the social perception of automobile accidents and slaughter. Insofar as one can calculate in advance the number of dead and maimed for each weekend, each day, automobile accidents are more than accidents. They form a part of the murderous necessity that keeps the coffers filled: private automobiles over public transportation, highways over railroads are not merely consumer choice; they are dictated by a social reality which in the drive toward surplus value has dictated the choices. A rational and human mode of transportation would threaten capitalist accumulation, so an irrational mode is preserved.

This is a social and real configuration of inhumanity against which the single human individual is helpless. Yet aside from minor and insignificant improvements in safety design, one assumes the driver is at fault. In the same breath as we are told how many are to die this weekend we are told to drive especially carefully, as if the latter had any effect on the former. It does not. The accidents are no accidents. They are embedded in the social reality; accidents are a form of necessity under conditions of unfreedom.[36] The response is "humanistic": an appeal to the driver to heed the road and not the social processes that recklessly manufacture the accidents. Attention to the latter may do more than take the driver's attention off the road; it might suggest that safety lies in collective action: dismantling a dangerous society.

Using the same approach, the humanists would have it that alienation is a problem of human sensitivity and is not extruded from the bourgeois mode of production. Rogers in *Encounter Groups* writes that "the encounter group movement will be a growing counterforce to the dehumanization of our culture." Proposed is not the dissolution of dehumanization but its humanization. The brutal totality is accepted as given; unacceptable are only some of the joints that squeak and groan, annoying light sleepers. The blindness toward the reality that desensitizes, the fixation on incidentals, expose the ideological content of the sensitivity. One is sensitive toward the immediate and indifferent toward the more distant social forces which define the immediate. "One of the most imaginative uses [of encounter groups] has been in dealing with the psychological problems that develop when two companies merge," writes Rogers.[37] The unholy alliance between monopoly capital and the Center for Studies of the Person is no sacrilege. The concern of the former for pacifying its employees, like the concern of the latter, is not malicious but is grounded in the lie of bourgeois society that they both share: the ills are subjective. The objective whole is driven from mind by a program of "feel more, think less." The "imaginative" use of sensitivity to aid monopolization is *Realpolitik;* sensitivity turns out to be the grim business of helping business against the hapless individual. That the intent is otherwise changes nothing. The individual is led to believe that with a little self-help alienation will be washed down the drain like dirt in a sparkling sink. Rogers's *Encounter Groups* for all its sensitivity and testimonies — and because of them — is copy for the campaign of self-manipulation in an age of mass manipulation.

The attitude of Rogers, and others, toward the concept and fact of "role" crystallizes the difference between a positive humanism and a dialectical one. To them the concept and fact of roles are a violation of humanity. The role is a façade, consciously assumed so as to hide the real self. "In an intensive group experience it is often possible for a person to peep within himself and see the loneliness of the real being who lives inside his everyday shell or role." The notion here is simple: the real person is locked within the artificial, the role, and needs a little encouragement to step out into the fresh air. As with the neo-Freudians, society is conceived as an external factor, an outside force acting on the individual, but not decisively casting the individual from without and from within. This mechanical conception, severing within and without, and presupposing that only the outside is prey to social forces, is assumed or stated throughout the post-Freudian writings. Their humanism derives from the insistence that roles are an alienated mode of behavior.

Critical theory goes further than the post-Freudians. It admits what the humanists in their impatience to find humanity everywhere deny: that roles are not only fraudulent, they are also real. Roles are not merely adopted by the subject as a façade that can be dropped with a little willpower. They are an alienated mode of behavior custom-fit for an alienated society. The neat division between roles and real selves reduces society to a masquerade party. Yet not even plastic surgery can heal the psychic disfigurements. The social evil reaches into the living fibers; people not only assume roles, they are roles. This admission is no concession to inhumanity. Rather, in articulating the full strength of the prevailing inhumanity it holds forth the hope of its material transcendence. The insistence, on the other hand, on finding humanity everywhere by underestimating the objective and social foundation of inhumanity perpetuates the latter — it humanizes inhumanity.

Critical theory seeks to preserve both moments in their contradiction: roles as true and false. They are true insofar as they are not merely a paper-thin façade, but are inextricably entangled with the individual; and false insofar as they are the mode of behavior of an unfree society. For this reason a psychology or sociology of roles is not simply to be rejected as inhuman and brutal; rather it testifies to the real processes of this society that annihilate the individual and autonomy. Yet to the degree that such a psychology or sociology is *unconscious,* that is, to the degree that it accepts roles as natural and human and not estranged human behavior, it is ideological. "The concept of role, lifted without analysis from the social façade, helps perpetuate the monstrosity of role-playing itself." [38]

The reflex rejection of role psychology and kindred methods of rat and behavioral psychology as violations of the human spirit is, however, no less ideological.[39] These types of psychology and sociology mirror the actual inhumanity of reality. Rat psychology is human psychology where a total society has trained human beings to be creatures of stimulus and response, i.e., rats. "Insofar as the hardening of society has reduced men more and more to objects . . ." wrote Adorno, "methods which convey this are no sacrilege. The unfreedom of the method serves freedom in that it wordlessly testifies to the prevailing unfreedom." [40] Or as Adorno and Horkheimer wrote in another context: "The usual objection that empirical social research is too mechanical, too crude, and too unspiritual [*ungeistig*] shifts the responsibility from that which science is investigating to science itself. The much-castigated inhumanity of empirical methods still is more humane than the humanizing of the inhuman." [41]

This last refers to the idealistic misconception of the humanist protesting roles, behavioral methods, and the like; it shifts the evil from the social conditions that coerce men and women into standardized roles onto the social science that is merely registering these conditions. Its inhumanity consists in that instead of changing the conditions that dehumanize, it is satisfied with a change in method, as if by humanist rhetoric alone the inhuman conditions will be dissolved. In his discussion of the method of classification and typology used in *The Authoritarian Personality*, Adorno wrote:

> Individualism, opposed to inhuman pigeonholing, may ultimately become a mere ideological veil in a society which actually *is* inhuman and whose intrinsic tendency towards "subsumption" of everything shows itself by the classification

of people themselves. In other words the critique of typology should not neglect the fact that large numbers of people are no longer or rather never were "individuals." [42]

The point, then, is not to unconsciously use role methodology which takes as natural the result of an unnatural process. It is to use the procedure, if at all, critically. Already Marx used the term "character mask" to mean not that men and women were mechanically divided into role and authentic self, but that character was the precipitation of extra-individual social forces that penetrated the individual.[43] As Adorno wrote of the typology used in *The Authoritarian Personality*, it is *"critical* typology in the sense that it comprehends the typification of men itself as a social function."

That the blank espousal of individuality and humanism, on the one hand, and a scientific behavioral psychology, on the other, leave little to choose shows well enough the contemporary configuration of these alternatives. Behaviorism à la Skinner of *Beyond Freedom and Dignity* would phase out as unscientific freedom and individuality for new and improved behavior modification. The progressive note here is the materialistic accent. Skinner disdains the spiritualities and abstractions that are the stuff of the humanists. What he writes of alienation could have been written by a socialist. "The fact that young people drop out of school, refuse to get jobs . . . is not due to feelings of alienation but to defective social environments." [44] Yet the progressive and confident materialism degenerates into the insoluble contradictions of positivism. Skinner accepts the ideology of freedom and individuality as if it were the motor of history and not its ideology; in analyzing the social disorder he shifts the blame to the ideology. With the courage of his logic, then, he decrees the opposite: the abolition of freedom by way of behavior modification and a souped-up environment, in the name of a new "scientific" value — survival. The irony is that freedom and individuality have only existed in their mangled bourgeois form; to propose junking them in the name of survival is to propose the very society we now have, one that subsists exactly by an ethos of survival, paying lip service to freedom and the individual while rewarding the victors and punishing the victims. Freedom and individuality have never been more than adornments for an ugly environment of survival of the fittest. To go *beyond* them can only mean to realize them; otherwise, to go beyond is only to further sink into a society that reduced them to lies in the first place.[45]

Appropriately the protest against this materialism in the name of humanity comes from an ideologue of the establishment that daily wrongs humanity.[46] The sham indignation of a former vice-president of the republic toward a behaviorism that threatens the sanctity of the individual is sustained only by the "big lie" technique: even a glimmer of the truth is too much. Here, too, the ideology of freedom and individuality is accepted as truth itself, only with different conclusions. We are to suppose that reality does not exist and that those who have suggested that individuals could be modified were the very first to dream it up. In truth individuals have been modified and manipulated for a long time, and the alibi has often been freedom and individuality. The contradictions of ideology and reality are resolved by these two alternatives, differently but identically. The latter, with the ax of law and order, would keep the lies coming so as to forget a reality that gives the lie to the lies; the behaviorist would give up the ideology so as to repair a reality that needs it no longer.

The humanist psychology is conformist in essence and trappings; it is the ideology of liberation of a one-dimensional society. Such psychology has forgotten what it never knew: the psychoanalytic, social, and political theory of the "heroic" era of bourgeois thought. Succumbing with enthusiasm to the social amnesia, it repeats the adages of an age as if they were discoveries of the future. Nothing is lacking in their writings; one can find, in the sage of the self-actualizing personality, Maslow, advice on how to defeat the Russians, praise of the capitalist entrepreneur, and more. He tells us in *Eupsychian Management,* a book an admirer calls "Maslow's reply to *Das Kapital*," [47] how to figure out whether a job with a higher salary which entails leaving one's home and friends is worth the move. "I have asked myself how much money is it worth to me to give up my friendship with my best friends.... If, for instance, I arbitrarily assign a value of $1,000 a year to having an intimate friend (which is certainly a modest figure), then this new job which has been offered at a raise of, let's say, $2,000 or $3,000 or $4,000 a year simply is not what it looked like at first. I may actually be losing value, or dollar value." [48] This is the thinking, language, and style of domination. Values are dollar values, how to get the most from a buck. What Marx once wrote of Bentham, that he was a genius of bourgeois stupidity, could be said of Maslow — except that Maslow is no genius.

What is new in such formulations is not that friendship can be figured in dollars and cents, but the supreme confidence that such reasoning is the very quintessence of humanism. To maintain this fraud is possible only by the feat of forgetting that the post-Freudians have performed effortlessly. The facility with which they present barren comments as wisdom cannot be explained by personal defects; rather it is derived from the movement of society that is squeezing out of existence autonomous mind and thought. What is happening is not only the decline of thought, but its repression.

IV

Negative Psychoanalysis and Marxism

A beggar dreamt of a millionaire. As
he awoke he met a psychoanalyst. The
latter explained to him the millionaire
was a symbol for his father. "Curious,"
remarked the beggar.

HEINRICH REGIUS
(MAX HORKHEIMER), 1934 [1]

If subjectivism is the ill of conformist psychology, an anti-subjective objectivity has cursed Marxism. The categories of the individual, psyche, subjectivity have been cast off as immaterial, figuratively and literally, to the material and objective analysis of society. In recent years, Marxists and neo-Marxists have sought to rectify this; yet the very terms of this correction, "Marx and Freud," "historical materialism and psychoanalysis," "sociology and psychology," have exuded a positivistic and mechanistic approach. This manner of posing the problem suggests that the task is to make agreeable the incompatible by a round-table discussion that tables the contradictions. A harmonious synthesis of Marxism and psychoanalysis presupposes that society is without the antagonisms that are its essence. "True pluralism," wrote Max Horkheimer, "belongs to the concept of a future society." [2] This one is rent and torn, fractured at its source. Instead of ideologically synchronizing contradictions, or assigning them to separate halls of the academy, critical theory seeks to articulate them; the

73

task is not to homogenize the insolubles, but, as it were, to culture the differences.

To culture the differences entails pursuing two different logics simultaneously, the logic of society and the logic of the psyche. As noted in the preface, the history of this effort has not been a happy one. Those seeking to work out the relationship between Marxism and psychoanalysis have not been immune to the intellectual division of labor that severs the life nerve of dialectical thought. The various efforts to interpret Marx and Freud have been plagued by reductionism: the inability to retain the tension between individual and society, psychology and political economy.[3] Even Wilhelm Reich, the most dedicated of the Marx-Freud theoreticians, did not escape reductionism. What is necessary is the preservation without reification of this tension. "Psychoanalysis and historical materialism must co-exist." [4] They are fractured pieces of a fractured society. The reduction of a social constellation to an individual and instinctual one is as inadmissible as the reverse, the obliteration of the individual in a supraindividual sociology. More precisely this supraindividual sociology is the reverse; psychologism and sociologism are different sides of the coin of exchange value.

The two logics, the logics of society and psyche, begin to intersect in the 1920s because the logic of Marxism itself was then in the process of being rethought and reformulated. The story of this rethinking of Marxism can only be suggested here; it was spurred by the collapse of the Marxist party and movement — especially German Social Democracy — in the years following World War I. The analysis of this collapse and failure was inseparable from an analysis and critique of the failure of Marxism itself. As crystallized in the works of Georg Lukács and Karl Korsch this critique suggested that the lethal defect in the prevailing Marxism was its "mechanical" or "automatic" quality; it had conceived of social change as the changing of blueprints. Exactly what was lacking was the subjective, human, and philosophical content of Marxism. The efforts of Lukács and Korsch, and after them others such as the Frankfurt School, were toward salvaging this lost dimension of Marxism: subjectivity.

The attempt of Marxists to "think Freud" has been defined by the continued failure of the European revolution, or the continued success of bourgeois society. The objective conditions for revolution seemed "ripe" long ago. "For the revolutionary conditions have always been ripe." [5] The weak link in Marxism was the iron link in bourgeois society: subjectivity. "In the fateful months after November 1918, when the organized political power of the bourgeoisie was smashed and outwardly there was nothing else in the way of the transition from capitalism to socialism," wrote Karl Korsch about the brief revolutionary period in post-World War I Germany, "the great chance was never seized because the *socio-psychological* preconditions for its seizure were lacking." [6] It was these "socio-psychological preconditions" — the subjective moment — that became the focus for the left Freudians such as Reich.

From the start the pursuit of subjectivity within Western Marxism was couched in the negative: it was directed toward fathoming why subjectivity did *not* show, why the "great chance" was lost, and bourgeois society kept grinding on. It sought to explain, as it were, why there was "no" subjectivity, and, at the same time, to awaken the subject to thought and action. To do this necessitated exploring the nature of the subject, not dismissing it, as doctrines of automatic, mechanical social change did and do. Insofar as these doctrines are subject-*less*, they could not comprehend the dialectic of social change. Reich wrote in an autobiographical account of an abortive demonstration of some two hundred Communists in Vienna in 1928:

> These two hundred Communists believed that when industry *objectively* collapses, when wages are *objectively* reduced and when the simplest freedom strivings are *objectively* repressed — that these things must automatically and self-

evidently incite the people to revolutionary indignation. The whole of revolutionary politics in Germany and Austria until 1933 was built upon this idea. This thinking was wrong.[7]

As is well known, to the Russian Communist orthodoxy the unofficial project of Western Marxism of revitalizing a lost moment of Marxism — subjectivity and philosophy — smacked of heresy. Those who were part of this effort such as Lukács and Korsch were forced to submit or forced out. The Russian reaction to Freud and Freudians, after an initial period, was no more friendly.[8] What is more, the conscientious defenders of Soviet Marxism discovered an internal relationship between the heretics. W. Jurinetz, in one of the first substantial Russian critiques of Freud, in 1925, mentioned Lukács's errors and in the same breath denounced the Freudians for subjectivity. Jurinetz charged the Freudians with subjectivity, decadence, and aestheticism; he observed that the subjective and intellectual style of the aesthete was also "noticeable in Lukács. . . . All his other errors have their roots here."[9]

Jurinetz was on to something; yet the similarity of the efforts is as important as the distinction. If the similarity is derived from an exploration of subjectivity, the distinction is defined by *two dimensions* of subjectivity: the philosophical (or historical) and the psychological. Neither Lukács nor Korsch studied this second dimension. The above citation from Korsch on the absent "socio-psychological preconditions" for revolution is misleading; these preconditions are interpreted by Korsch in nonpsychological or only neopsychological terms. According to him, what is lacking is the "belief" in the practicability of socialism; this in turn is derived from the "backwardness of socialist *theory* vis-a-vis all problems of the practical realization" of socialism.[10] Even within the heresy, Korsch here remains orthodox in the allegiance to a nonpsychological dimension of subjectivity. The psychic dimension is lost or, at least, diluted in its translation into theoretical questions on the practical content of socialism.

If Lukács grants the existence of a psychic dimension, it is only so as to dismiss it. He strictly separates a philosophical from a psychic dimension, giving a political reading of the psychic one as contingent and empirical; as such he considers it the source for revisionism and opportunism. To Lukács a psychological consciousness is an immediate and positivist one — a consciousness that remains within the grip of bourgeois society; it lacks theory. "Class consciousness is identical with neither the psychological consciousness of individual members of the proletariat nor the (mass-psychological) consciousness of the proletariat as a whole; but it is, on the contrary, *the sense become conscious of the historical role of the class.*" It is exactly revisionism and opportunism that confused the two. "Opportunism *mistakes the actual psychological state of consciousness of the proletariat for the class consciousness of the proletariat.*" It seeks to "*reduce class consciousness . . . of the proletariat to the level of the psychologically given.*" [11]

To Marxists schooled in psychoanalysis, it is this very cleavage between the dimensions of history and psychology that seems questionable; it openly ignores any dialectic between a psychological and historical consciousness. If this is the heretical introduction of subjectivity into Marxism it remains too traditional; stripped of its psychic content it is a paper-thin subjectivity. Lacking a psychic dimension, the subject turns abstract, distant from the actual carnal and psychic individual. To be sure, these formulations were also Lukács's strength: the deliberate repudiation of a nonhistorical psychological consciousness bearing the imprint of bourgeois society. But it was also his weakness; the nondialectical flight from the empirical and psychological subject exhausted itself in bad abstractions. The abyss between the abstractions and the empirical reality could only be bridged by the party. Hence it has recently been argued that Lukács's fetish of the party follows from his neglect of the psychological subjective moment.[12]

Critical theory does not know a sharp break between these two dimensions; they are neither rendered identical nor absolutely severed. In its pursuit of this dialectical relationship it has resisted the two forms of positivism that lose the tension: psychologism and sociologism. If the specific tendency of bourgeois and liberal thought has been toward psychologism — the reduction of social concepts to individual and psychological ones — the specific tendency of socialist and Marxist thought has been toward the opposite: the reduction of individual concepts to a desiccated notion of history and society. Both flatten out a society-individual antagonism, the former in favor of an abstract notion of the individual, the latter, of an abstract notion of society. To be sure, psychologism remains false in all its forms, while sociologism at least pays respect to society as the determining structure. "In the face of the present impotence of the individual — all individuals — what is primary in explaining social processes and tendencies is society and sciences concerned with society: sociology and economics." [13]

Yet if sociologism does not err at first in underestimating the force and power of society, it errs at second. In sidestepping the psychic structure of the individual, it photographs without penetrating society; it does not peel away so as to reach society's deeper reign over the individual. It gets the picture but not the essence. A specific problem for Western Marxism is the perpetuation of an obsolete social system; to be analyzed is why a revolutionary subject does not act or appear. "Since the market economy was shattered, and patched up provisionally until the next crisis, its laws do not suffice for its explanation; other than by psychology, in which the objective compulsion is continually and newly internalized, it is not understandable either why men passively adjust to a condition of unchanged destructive irrationality or why they enroll in movements whose contradiction to their own interests is in no way difficult to perceive." [14] Sociologism underestimates the primacy of society by not exploring its depth relations with and over the individual; it banalizes society to a surface phenomenon. [15]

A convergence takes place between the liberal psycho-analytic revisions of the neo-Freudians and the antipsycho-analytic Marxism. Both suffer from sociologism, the former unwittingly and the latter knowingly. The Russian ortho-doxy exorcised subjectivity; the psychoanalytic revisionists deliberately add it. Both, however, lose it. Soviet Marxism, dismissing subjectivity from the start, ends with a con-tentless notion of society. The neo-Freudians in their eager-ness to find the role of society do not get past the surface and end with a vapid notion of society. Again, regardless of their own politics, it has been Freud and his followers who, in their stubborn pursuit of the genesis and structure of the individual psyche, have testified to the power of society in and over the individual. This is the authentic dialectic of psychoanalysis; apparently the opposite of the universal (society), psychoanalysis rediscovers society in the individual monad. The critical edge of psychoanalysis is rooted in this dialectic: it pierces the sham of the iso-lated individual with the secret of its socio-sexual-biologi-cal substratum. "Freudian psychology does not so much capitulate to the appearance of individuality, as it funda-mentally destroys it as only a philosophical and social concept can do." [16] Depth psychology, by its own logic, turns into sociology and history.

Sociologism prematurely cuts off an exploration of subjectivity in the name of society, which it can no longer understand without subjectivity; critical theory, drawing upon psychoanalysis, sinks into subjectivity till it hits bot-tom: society. It is here where subjectivity devolves into objectivity; subjectivity is pursued till it issues into the social and historical events that preformed and deformed the subject. This constitutes the subject-object dialectic — a dialectic which is a violation of the logic of positivism, shared by both psychological behaviorists and their op-ponents, "humanist" psychologists. This positivist logic alternatively proscribes subjectivity (as nonscientific) or recommends it (as nonscientific, a human value). Both variants of positivism accept a vacant notion of the subject, only they appraise it differently. Before the gaze of critical theory the illusion that the subject is purely subjective becomes transparent; it sees through to the objective content of subjectivity. "Subjectivity itself is to be brought to objectivity; its movements are not to be banished from cognition." [17] To bring subjectivity to objectivity entails teaching it how to speak about what it bespeaks: society and history. Such an effort is an objective theory of subjectivity.

An objective theory of subjectivity is "twice" objective; not only does it explore subjectivity till it reveals its social and objective determinants, but it reveals a society that had administered the subject out of existence. Again, Marxism, at least since Lukács and Korsch, explores subjectivity; but a (revolutionary) subject that does not appear. Hence the theory of subjectivity is also a theory of bourgeois society that eradicated the subject. The individual is deindividualized, rendered subject-less. "In bourgeois society capital is independent and has individuality, while the living person is dependent and has no individuality." [18] A critical theory of subjectivity to be adequate to this reality is consciously contradictory; it pursues subjectivity till, so to speak, it disappears; its psychoanalysis is negative: a theory of a subject-less subject — or a not yet liberated subjectivity.

Such a theory is to be distinguished from positive psychologies — theories of ego formation, identity, growth, and so on, that assume what is yet to be created: the individual. Negative psychoanalysis is psychoanalysis in the era of synchronized capitalism; it is the theory of the individual in eclipse. It is psychoanalysis just to its own field of inquiry, the individual, in the period of the disintegration of the ego under the impact of a massified society. Negative psychoanalysis is "twice" objective in that it traces at first the objective content of subjectivity, and second, discovers there is only an objective configuration to subjectivity. Today there is "no" subjectivity.

Here as elsewhere the way out is through. "The overpowering of the subject by the object, which hinders it from becoming a subject, hinders it just so from knowledge of the object."[19] This overpowering by a brutal reality which has left the individual numb and dumb is to be overcome, at least in thought and theory, before subjectivity can be realized: insight into the very material and social conditions that mutilate it. Before the individual can exist, before it can become an individual, it must recognize to what extent it does not yet exist. It must shed the illusion of the individual before becoming one. Subjectivity must be brought to objectivity so it can be realized. This is the nub of the matter. "Criticism has plucked the imaginary flower from the chain not so that man will wear the chain without any fantasy or consolation, but so that he will shake off the chain and cull the living flower."[20]

A further clarification: smuggled into the term subjectivity, as used in this chapter, is a crucial ambiguity; it seems to refer at the same time to two very different phenomena: the proletariat as a (potential) subject of history and the bourgeois subject as the problematic individual tossed up by the market. This ambiguity is one of reality, and is not merely conceptual; the very problem is defined by the fact that the specific qualities of the proletariat which, to follow Lukàcs, steer it in the direction of class consciousness are (temporarily?) overlaid with specific bourgeois properties that dissolve class consciousness. The concepts *do* span the classes, but this is caused by the failure of the specific proletariat properties to emerge. The class with "radical chains" is also restrained by a bourgeois chain that gives it freedom of movement without freedom.

An example may sharpen this. At first it may seem misleading to speak of the eclipse of the individual as if this were true of both the bourgeoisie and the proletariat — an eclipse of subjectivity per se. Theoretically, in Marxism, the proletariat was never composed of (bourgeois) individuals; this was a luxury reserved for the wealthier. However, again, the very problem is that the form of individuality that prevails in the bourgeoisie is not confined to the bourgeoisie; rather it seeps into the proletariat and cripples the process of the proletariat which seeks to constitute itself as the historical subject.

Why this process occurs, and how reversible or deeply embedded it is in the proletariat, cannot be discussed here. Important only is that the concepts that seem to blur the distinction between classes are not to be explained away, or denied, by the mere affirmation that capitalism is a class society. This is true, but the concepts gain their truth from the dynamic of capitalism that within a class structure works to level; concretely, this means that late capitalism tends to erase the specific and unique secondary qualities of the proletariat that seem to be the precondition for class consciousness. A proletariat that is partially composed of bourgeois individuals is undoubtedly a contradiction, but it is a contradiction of reality, not simply of concepts.

Within the revolutionary theory as derived from Lukàcs the political content of negative psychoanalysis is found; to the point that a subject does not develop, the revolutionary process is thrown into doubt, for the shift and reversal of bourgeois history does not take place. An automatic process — that is a mechanical one without a subject — can only update the existing society. To change directions necessitates a historical and conscious intervention.[21] What does not derive from Lukàcs is an adequate exploration of the failure of the subject's intervention. This may in part stem from the other dimension of subjectivity: the psychological. Aside from the external social and material conditions, counterrevolution may be embedded in the revolutionaries themselves — a form of *psychic reification*. Marcuse has stated this most emphatically: past revolutions seem to proceed to a certain point "from which the transition to new, not only quantitatively, but qualitatively different conditions would perhaps proceed. At this point the revolution is usually vanquished and domination is internalized, reestablished, and continued at a higher level." Following Freud, "We can raise the question whether alongside the socio-historical Thermidor that can be demonstrated in all past revolutions, there is not also a *psychic* Thermidor . . . Is there perhaps in the individuals themselves already a dynamic at work that *internally* negates possible liberation and gratification and that supports external forces of denial?" [22] Or as Marcuse put it elsewhere:

> In every revolution there seems to have been a historical moment when the struggle against domination might have been victorious — but the moment passed. An element of *self-defeat* seems to be involved in this dynamic (regardless of the validity of such reasons as the prematurity and inequality of forces).[23]

It should be noted to what extent the reformulations that sought to introduce into Marxism a psychological moment of subjectivity, and implicitly or explicitly were critiques of a vulgar automatic Marxism, were enunciated by Freud himself. Evidently Freud was not arguing from a left position; if he could write that the Russian Revolution was a "tremendous experiment," a "message of a better future," [24] he could also state: "In spite of all my dissatisfaction with the present economic system I have no hope that the road pursued by the Soviets will lead to improvement. Indeed any such hope that I may have cherished has disappeared in this decade of Soviet rule. I remain a liberal of the old school." [25]

Yet his critique of communism had two parts. First, he denied that the destructive drive could be practically eradicated.[26] The other objection, however, was directed against the narrow materialistic base of Marxism. To Freud the superego was rooted in parents, earlier education, etc.; it was a tool of the past anchored in the present.

> It seems likely that what are known as materialist views of history sin in underestimating this factor. They brush it aside with the remark that human "ideologies" are nothing

other than the product and superstructure of their contemporary economic conditions. This is true, but very probably not the whole truth. Mankind never lives entirely in the present. The past . . . lives on in the ideologies of the superego and yields only slowly to the influences of the present and to new changes; and so long as it operates through the super-ego it plays a powerful part in human life, independently of economic conditions.[27]

The provocative extract of a 1937 letter that Jones published should be considered here; in it Freud responds to a criticism of his comprehension of Marx. "I know that my comments on Marxism are no evidence either of a thorough knowledge or of a correct understanding of the writings of Marx and Engels. I have since learned — rather to my satisfaction — that neither of them has denied the influence of ideas and super-ego factors. *That invalidates the main contrast between Marxism and psychoanalysis which I had believed to exist.*" [28]

Probably the first and most directly political effort to seek out the psychological grounds of self-defeat belongs to Paul Federn's work from 1919 *Zur Psychologie der Revolution: Die vaterlose Gesellschaft,* an interpretation of the contemporary German revolution. Federn, who was a student of Freud and a socialist,[29] suggested that a deeply embedded patriarchal authoritarian attitude which is encased even in socialist organizations has kept bourgeois society on its tracks. "The general father complex was responsible for the fact that the social order has so long been able to maintain itself." If this complex is not dissolved, revolutionary progress is in doubt. "It is very possible that despite the devastation by the war, the patriarchal order will be able to solve the technical problems of rebuilding a new economy if the psychic preconditions, the unconscious subsumption under the father-son relation, does not cease." [30]

What is unique in Federn's work is that he translated these formulations into the political reality; his work is a critique of social democracy as it perpetuates the father-son relation and, further, is a defense of "councils," which create a new ethos of brothers (and sisters?) and finally abolish the father-son society. "All previous organizations were organized from the leader down; the organizational pyramid provided the father-son relation with an ideal form.... The new organization — the council — grows out of the masses, out of the base, and from the base it receives the impulse and invisible psychic system: the relation of the brother." [31]

Yet Federn was pessimistic about the possibility that the new ethos would be victorious; too much of the old society worked against it. Like Reich after him, Federn stressed the importance of the family in implanting the patriarchal attitudes, and the difficulty of extirpating them. "The congruence of the family with the fallen patriarchal-based state of the Kaiser and its incongruence with an organization of brothers is the only authentic psychological problem in the construction of a non-patriarchal order of society." The very depths of this anchoring left Federn in doubt as to whether a society of brothers can be yet achieved. He closed on a pessimistic note: "The father-son complex has suffered the greatest defeat. Yet from the family education and inherited feeling it is deeply rooted in mankind; and it probably this time also will prevent a complete victory of the fatherless society." [32]

Federn's analysis was not pursued, if only because the political situation would not again lend itself to a favorable psychoanalytic interpretation of a revolutionary upsurge. Rather the accent fell on a psychological mechanism that sustained the ongoing capitalist system and blocked class consciousness and the historical subjectivity. As with Federn, a specific relationship was emphasized, the authoritarian one of father and son; with Reich, Fromm, the Frankfurt School, this was generalized into the notion of "character." For Marxists character seemed to concretely express the mediation between the individual instincts and the social necessities.

In Reich's and Fromm's work of the early 1930s, character is a precipitation of the intersection of the individual psyche and society; a significant vehicle for imprinting character is the family. Psychoanalytic characterology, wrote Fromm in a 1932 essay "Psychoanalytic Characterology and Its Relevance for Social Psychology," first published in the Frankfurt School journal, "can serve as the starting point for a social psychology that will show how the character traits common to most members of a society are conditioned by the distinctive nature of that society. This social influence on character formation operates first and foremost through the family." [33] Freud overlooked, Fromm wrote in the Frankfurt School collection *Autorität und Familie* (1936), that "the family in the first place represents particular social content, and through its mediation ... in the production of socially necessary mental structure lies its most important social function." [34] Or as Reich wrote in *Character Analysis* (1933), "Every social order creates those character forms which it needs for its preservation." In other words, "The character structure ... is the crystallization of the sociological process of a given epoch." [35] According to *Geschlechtsreife, Enthaltsamkeit, Ehemoral* (1930), the family is the specific instrument of education of bourgeois society; "It is the mediator between the economic structure of bourgeois society and its ideological superstructure." [36]

The Frankfurt School followed the drift of this analysis: to search out psychic mechanisms, such as character structure, that thwarted class consciousness. Horkheimer wrote in 1932, "That men preserve economic relations which they have outgrown in force and need, instead of replacing them through a higher and more rational form of organization, is possible only because the actions of a numerically significant social stratum are not determined by cognition, but by an instinctual motive force that falsifies consciousness. In no way do mere ideological maneuvers form the root of this historically important moment ... on the contrary, the psychic structure of these groups, that is the character of their members, is constantly renewed in connection with their role in the economic process." [37] Or as Horkheimer put it later, "Force in its naked form is in no way sufficient to explain why a dominated class so long endures the yoke; it is especially insufficient in periods when the economic apparatus is ripe for a better system of production, the culture is in dissolution, and the property relations and existing forms of life in general overtly become a fetter to social forces." To understand this one need know the "psychic composition of men in various social groups." The family is again crucial. "The family as one of the most important agents of education concerns itself with the reproduction of human character ... and largely imparts to human characters the authoritarian attitudes on which the bourgeois order depends." [38]

The notion of character was carried through to later Frankfurt School works, most notably the more academic *The Authoritarian Personality.* If the questions posed differed from the earlier ones, both the answers settled on character structure and the family as instruments of social mediation — one in the context of a delayed revolution, the other in the context of potential fascism. However, in *The Authoritarian Personality* the sociological and political element seemed to be hidden. The danger of psychologism loomed. Adorno in his scientific "autobiography" noted a misconception about *The Authoritarian Personality* which because of "its emphasis was not entirely unjustified: that the authors had sought to analyze anti-semitism, together with fascism solely subjectively, and had fallen into the error that political-economic phenomena were primarily psychological." But, responded Adorno, "in contradiction to certain economic orthodoxy" they had not been "inflexible" toward psychology, but sought it as a "moment of enlightenment.... Yet we have never doubted the primacy of objective factors over psychological.... We saw socio-psychology as a subjective mediation of an objective social system: without its mechanism the subject would not be able to be held on the leash." [39]

The notion of character as a necessary form of dehumanization distinguishes the Frankfurt School notion from that employed by the neo-Freudians and others. With the Frankfurt School, character participates in the dialectic of "second nature"; it is historical as the product of a specific society; and it is "natural" as an unconscious phenomenon which inexorably follows laws and patterns. Character, like personality, is a form of unfreedom.[40] Against the neo-Freudians, who consider character a harmonious totality, Adorno interprets it as a result of a series of "shocks" inflicted on the individual; it bespeaks oppression and violence, not growth, choice, and values. "The character which they, the revisionists, hypostatize is to a much greater extent the result of such shocks." The totality of the character is false: "One could almost call it a system of scars, which are only integrated — and never entirely — under suffering." Or character is the result of "the reification of real experience."[41]

Character is another form of the suppression and molding of the autonomous individual in bourgeois society. It refers to the same process that renders narcissism the prevailing form of individualism: the ego regresses into unconsciousness; it becomes automatic. The ego's "reactions to the outside world and to the instinctual desires emerging from the id," writes Marcuse, "become increasingly 'automatic.' The conscious processes of confrontation are replaced to an increasingly large degree by immediate, almost physical reactions. . . . It is as though the free space which the individual has at his disposal for his psychic process has been greatly narrowed down; it is no longer possible for something like an individual psyche to develop. . . . This reduction of the relatively autonomous ego is empirically observable in people's frozen gestures." This whole process Marcuse calls *"the reification and automatization of the ego."*[42]

For orthodox and Russian Marxists a suspicion was raised by these formulations: the suspicion of subjectivity or psychologism; the reduction of social analysis to individual analysis, revolution to therapy. Crude mechanical Marxism found no place for the subject; it patterned social change on a quasi-automatic process. This was the inner relationship between the German Social Democracy and the Stalinist orthodoxy, and this is why both resisted the reinterpretation of Marxism centered around Lukács and Korsch that sought to save a philosophical subjective dimension. The introduction of a psychic dimension of subjectivity seemed to suggest that the ills of society could be cured by curing the ills of the individual. The suspicion was not entirely unfounded. The critique of Jurinetz that found a relationship between Lukács and the Freudians was inspired by a book by Aurel Kolnai, *Psychoanalysis and Society,* that reveled in psychologisms. "Anarchism is the faithful social projection of the uterus." "Bolshevism is characterized by the withdrawal of inhibitions and repressions." [43]

Moreover, psychologism surfaced continually within psychoanalysis. Fritz Wittels presented to the Vienna Society a psychological analysis of a Russian revolutionary who had recently attempted a political assassination; absolutely no credence was given to a political context or motivation. Adler, then a social-democrat, protested: one cannot "follow Wittels in his opinion that, in a real event, the ideology can be totally divorced from what we call emotional life." [44] Even Freud agreed with Adler. "One must not condemn the assassins so harshly and unmask them because of unconscious motives. The unconscious motive deserves forebearance." [45]

The Marxists who were drawn to psychoanalysis were forced to carefully work out their theoretical positions, so as to avoid the specific failing of psychoanalysis: psychologism. Their formulations, while remaining alert to the charge of subjectivism, implicitly or explicitly criticized a vulgar Marxism that ignored the individual and subject. Probably the most successful formulations belong to those of Reich and Otto Fenichel; but they were hardly alone. [46]

The efforts not only in Germany but elsewhere are numerous. Reich's are outstanding if only because he was the most active and prolific.[47] Reich worked to delineate the exact place of psychoanalysis within Marxism. In the terms used here, he explored the relationship between a psychic dimension of subjectivity and a historical one: how the former blocked the latter — ultimately the proletariat itself — from acting within the historical reality. At least in the beginning, he was very much alive to the dangers of psychologism. His 1929 essay, "Dialectical Materialism and Psychoanalysis" — in part a reply to Jurinetz's piece — stated that psychoanalysis possessed limited validity; it was restricted to the "psychological life of man in society . . . It cannot replace a sociological doctrine, nor can a sociological doctrine develop out of it." For this reason "The phenomenon of class consciousness is not accessible to psychoanalysis." [48]

The bulk of the essay was a critique of a vulgar materialism that maintained that "psychological phenomena do not exist: the life of the soul is simply a physical process." Citing Marx's thesis on Feuerbach that all previous materialism was defective in ignoring subjectivity or activity, Reich showed the incompatibility of simple materialism with Marxism; if the crude Marxist were "logical, one should not speak of class consciousness . . . but should wait until chemistry has supplied the necessary formula for the physical processes concerned, or until the science of reflexes has discovered the appropriate reflexes." Rather, within Marxism there was no one-to-one relation, no automatic, chemical, or mechanical cause and effect between the economic reality and the consciousness of the subjects.

Exactly here is where psychoanalysis intervenes: "Between the two terminal points — the economic structure of society at one end, the ideological superstructure at the other . . . psychoanalysis sees a number of intermediate stages." And exactly here it can play a role within Marxism, "at that point where psychological questions arise as a result of the Marxist thesis that materialist existence

transforms itself into 'ideas inside the head.'" Or psychoanalysis can clarify "the way that ideologies are formed
'inside the head.'"[49]

Other left Freudians of the period more or less followed
Reich's formulations. Fromm wrote in "Politik und Psychoanalyse" that psychoanalysis "can show in what manner
particular economic conditions influence the psychic apparatus of men and produce particular ideological results:
it can provide information on the 'how' of the dependence
of ideological facts on particular configurations."[50] Or as
Fromm wrote in an essay for the Frankfurt School journal,
historical materialism could do without psychology only
"where ideology was the *immediate* expression of economic interests." Otherwise, psychoanalysis can illuminate
"how the economic situation is transformed into ideology
via man's drives."[51] Similarly, Otto Fenichel would write
in an article for Reich's journal, "The economic conditions
do not just influence the individual directly, but also indi-
rectly, via a change in his psychic structure." Again,
psychoanalysis intervenes at the actual 'how' of this transformation: the transformation of the ideology into a force
in the individual.[52]

Neither the full content of Reich's work nor the stages
of his development can be discussed here. The emphasis
of his work shifted from the 1929 essay; it sought to un-
cover the concrete mediation by which ideology was mate-
rialized and anchored in the individual. This became urgent
with the political events; the question posed was why the
proletariat fell short of its revolutionary mission, or alternatively why it was susceptible to fascism. The family and
character structure moved to the center of the analyses.[53]

In the context here, perhaps Reich's most important
contribution, following the outlines of the theory of psychoanalysis and Marxism, was the notion of "reproduction."
Production referred to the cultural and ideological necessities that are concretely produced by the society, but
hang, so to speak, in the air; reproduction refers to the
manner and mode by which ideology is translated in the

everyday life and behavior of the individual. As Reich
described it, the ideology and repressive morality which
are at first derived from the property relations ultimately
result in the "inner acceptance of the morality by the mass
individual." This in turn becomes a social and reactionary
force: psychically reproduced ideology.

> This social morality, anchored in all individuals and repro-
> ducing itself permanently, has in this manner a reciprocal
> effect on the economic base in a conservative direction. The
> exploited person affirms the economic order which guaran-
> tees his exploitation; the sexually repressed person affirms
> even the sexual order which restricts his gratification and
> makes him ill, and he wards off any system that might cor-
> respond to his need. In this manner morality carries out its
> socio-economic assignment.[54]

The full extent of Reich's critique of crude Marxism is
best found in *The Mass Psychology of Fascism*. It shows
in microcosm the divergence between a dialectical Marxism and a mechanical one that eliminated subjectivity,
admitting only automatic progress in history. His first
words — "The German working class has suffered a serious
defeat" [55] — apparently earned him the wrath of the party
regulars.[56] They were a denial of the "revolutionary perspective" and recalled Trotskyist tendencies.[57] In a *Nachwort* (1934) to the second edition, where he noted that
the official Communist position is that the world is in the
midst of a revolutionary upsurge, Reich attacks as the
most "dangerous fetter" to German socialism "the unshakable belief in the natural necessity of socialist victory."
The social-democrats, crude Marxists, and others have
been unable to conceive the mediation of the subjective
and objective. The naive Marxists think that they can ignore men entirely, and, with a change in the economic
structure, the transformation of man will follow "almost
automatically." [58] To Reich it is necessary to recognize the

"cleavage" between the economic structure and the consciousness of the proletariat.

The usual Communist replies to Reich were not much above slander and slogans.[59] One of the better ones was by I. Sapir, in response to Reich's first essay "Psychoanalysis and Dialectical Materialism." Sapir did indicate one difficulty in Reich's position: Reich claimed that the question of class consciousness was inaccessible to psychoanalysis; yet he was theorizing about the problem of ideology formation, that is, the falsification of class consciousness. How could one separate the question of class consciousness from that of ideology? [60] In a response to this, Reich reformulated the relationship between psychoanalysis and Marxism. He wrote that the *blocks* to class consciousness were accessible to psychoanalysis; the more rational the behavior, that is, the more in tune with class consciousness, the less the need for psychological interpretations.[61]

A more important reply to Reich is to be found in Siegfried Bernfeld's response to Reich's critique of the death instinct. According to Reich, this reply was "officially" approved by Freud himself. At first Freud wanted Reich's essay to be published with an introductory note stating that it was written by a dedicated Communist. But because of opposition to this unprecedented editorial action in a psychoanalytic journal, Freud settled for a reply by Bernfeld which was published with Reich's essay. Bernfeld noted two things in passing that could suggest future differences between Reich and a critical psychology: Reich's 1) narrow materialism, and 2) positive notion of health. According to Bernfeld, Reich wanted to "purge psychoanalysis of 'metaphysical hypotheses' and restrict it to the clinical in the narrowest sense of the word." [62] Further, Reich pursued a "vague ideal of sexual health: full genitality, orgiastic potency, etc." [63]

If this was true in 1933, it was truer later. The attempt to remain loyal to a dialectical Marxism, shunning psychologism and sociologism, faltered; it was too great an effort. Reich began to succumb to the reification he sought to undo. He always stressed that psychoanalysis was a "natural science" and tended to define sexuality and health in terms of physiology. The positive description of the "genital character" in *Character Analysis* threatened to dissolve the social critique; [64] it was as if there could be healthy sexuality without a social transformation. These tendencies surfaced clearly and openly in an essay from 1935 on sexual economy. In this Reich claimed that his "sexual economy" is not "the product of the addition of Marxism and psychoanalysis." Rather, "The *kernel* of sex-economy theory, around which all further perceptions group . . . is my *orgasm theory*. This field of facts exists neither within the scope of Marx's economic teachings nor in analytic psychology; but rather concerns biological-physiological phenomena which exist in all things that live." The social critique narrows; capitalism "destroys orgastic potency"; and this Reich defined in purely mechanical terms: "a functional relation to *mechanical tension* . . . electric charge . . . electric discharge and mechanical relaxation. The completion of this series and its undisturbed function is the surest sign of a healthy psychic apparatus." [65]

It should be noted that it was exactly on this score, that critical theory — starting with Freud — dissociated itself from Reich. Freud, as early as 1928, in a letter to Lou Andreas-Salomé attacked Reich's fetish of genital sexuality. Freud called Reich "a worthy but impetuous young man, passionately devoted to his hobby horse, who now salutes in the genital orgasm the antidote to every neurosis." [66] Fromm, some years later in the Frankfurt School journal, criticized Reich's romanticizing of primitive sexuality.[67] Horkheimer would do the same, commenting on the "utopian meaning" which Reich ascribed to the release of genital sexuality.[68] Marcuse's remarks on Reich have followed these earlier ones.[69]

Reductionism of the psychological or sociological variety haunted psychoanalysis. Reich himself did not escape one form, nor the neo-Freudians another. Critical theory avoids the banalization of psychoanalysis by neither distending it to include all of society nor confining it to therapy and sexuality of the individual. Rather it has worked to preserve psychoanalysis as a critique in tension — a critique that transcends the individual but does not forget the individual in some suprahistorical psychological drama. Consciousness is not to be psychologized away as a waste product of individual neuroses or instincts, nor sociologized away as the prevailing social norms and values.

Otto Fenichel, once close to Reich and later to the Frankfurt School, sought to preserve both individual-instinctual and social components without reducing one to the other. His work illustrates critical theory's loyalty to the tension within psychoanalysis. (It has received little attention outside psychoanalytic circles, despite its sustained effort to resist reification and simplification.) Against interpretations that conceived of capitalism as derived from individual instincts, Fenichel stressed its social and extra-individual factors; against analyses that abstracted capitalism from the instinctual dynamic, Fenichel recalled its instinctual roots. Sandor Ferenczi, in "The Ontogenesis of the Interest in Money," traced the capitalist fascination with money to the child's interest in feces. "Pleasure in the intestinal contents becomes enjoyment of money, which, however . . . is seen to be nothing other than odorless, dehydrated filth that has been made to shine." [70] Fenichel in a response to Ferenczi, as well as to Géza Róheim and others prone to psychologism, argued in "The Drive to Amass Wealth" (1938) for a "reciprocal action" between instincts and the social configuration. "The instincts represent the general tendency, while matters of *money* and the desire to become wealthy represent a specific form which the general tendency can assume only in the presence of certain definite social conditions." "The existence of the erogenous pleasure in collection causes Ferenczi to overlook the fact that when the capitalist strives to increase his capital he does this on very rational grounds:

he is forced to it by competitors who produce on a larger scale. . . . A social system of this kind *makes use of* and strengthens erogenous drives that serve the necessity for accumulating. Of this there can be no doubt. There is considerable doubt, however, as to whether the existing economic conditions of production were created by the biological instinct." He wrote in conclusion, "Such a drive to become wealthy at one time did not exist and at some future time will exist no longer." [71]

Fenichel equally resisted the errors of Adlerians, neo-Freudians, and others who abstracted society from its biological and instinctual substrata and thereby attained a sham socialization of psychoanalysis.[72] In a review essay of Fromm's *Escape from Freedom,* Fenichel observed that the dynamic of instincts and society is lost, and the social moment that is advanced is idealized and spiritualized. "Instead of studying the interrelations of erogenous zones and object relationships, they [Fromm, Kardiner] think statically and are of the opinion that the insight into the role of object relationships contradicts the importance of erogenous zones." [73] The irony of the endeavor to escape from Freud's biologism is that it issues into real biologism — an abstract and contentless idealism which is ahistorical and invariant: biology. "Fromm gives examples of drives which came into existence at certain points of the historical development and thinks that this is an argument against Freud: the drive to 'enjoy nature's beauty' and 'the drive to work.' Certainly nobody will deny the social origin of these 'drives,' but their social origin does not contradict the assumption that deeper biological needs have been transformed into these 'new drives.' " Further, these drives become "very abstract and, in comparison with Freud's concrete analysis of the instinctual attitude, extremely vague." The "materialist advantage" of psychoanalysis is that it has shown that ideals such as truth and justice "are *not* [what Fromm considers them] 'genuine strivings,' but are formed out of biological needs by socially determined experiences." "It is not to be understood why an idealistic tendency to grow and develop should be regarded [as Fromm regards it] as 'biologically inherent in human nature' and sexual partial instincts should not." [74] Fenichel wrote elsewhere, in a review of a book by another neo-Freudian, Karen Horney: "Dr. Horney writes, 'My conviction expressed in a nutshell is that psychoanalysis should outgrow the limitations set by its being an instinctivistic and genetic psychology.' My conviction, expressed in a nutshell, is that the value of psychoanalysis as a natural scientific psychology is rooted in its being an instinctivistic and a genetic psychology." [75]

Fenichel's defense of psychoanalysis as a "genetic" science, that is, one focused on genesis and origins, can be pursued, for a moment, in a philosophical and theoretical dimension. This dimension can illuminate the nature of psychological and sociological reductionism, and it can cast light on the problem of consciousness as a psychic and/or historical phenomenon. These dimensions are inter-related. "The concept of the ego is dialectical," wrote Adorno, "both psychic and extra-psychic, a quantum of libido and the representative of outside reality." He also stated, "The bourgeoisie in its late phase is incapable of thinking genesis and validity in their simultaneous unity and difference." [76] These two statements are of one piece; they refer to different forms of positivist logic that can only flit between thinking exclusively about origins — psychologism — or exclusively about an abstract notion of truth and ideas.

Both are forms of reductionism, unable to preserve the dialectic of individual and society. One reduces all to the roots, e.g., capitalism to an instinct, and denies any truth that claims to go beyond its origin. Such teachings are to be found within psychoanalysis as well as elsewhere, as in varieties of sociology of knowledge. The equally blank approach disregards origins and accepts at face value claims to truth; this tilts over into pure idealism, as it refuses to acknowledge or study the contradiction between the historical substratum and the extrahistorical claims.

Again what is at issue is the nature of (class) consciousness and, in particular, the very relationship that most Marxists have ignored: the relationship between a psychological and historical dimension. If one defines consciousness exclusively by its subjective and psychological origin, then no particular form has any more claim to truth than any other; one has a model of society of self-interest groups all with equal demands — equally right and equally wrong. If consciousness is abstracted from its origin in reality, one is left with an idealistic notion of the battle of ideas uprooted from a carnal and psychic reality.

Adorno eschews both approaches. In his book on Husserl, he wrote, "The error of logical psychologism is that it wished to derive immediately out of psychic facts the validity of logical statements." Yet Husserl was equally wrong in his critique of logical psychologism; if he is right in disputing the "immediate identity ... of genesis and validity, he is wrong in hypothesizing their difference." [77] In his lectures on the theory of knowledge Adorno noted that, in response to psychologism, recent philosophy has relapsed into a form of Platonic realism. The precept "that the validity of the laws of thought is simply independent of the emergence of the ego ... is as false as the reverse precept ... that the laws of thought and laws of genesis are simply identical." [78] Or as he wrote elsewhere, "Genesis and validity are not to be separated without contradiction. Objective truth preserves the moment of its origin; the latter works permanently within it." [79]

Consciousness and thought are neither to be reduced to their subjective origin nor totally abstracted from it. The neo-Freudians, as some left Freudians, were unable to maintain this dialectic. Psychoanalysis itself was diluted — watered down into either a psychological technique for individual adjustment or a superficial theory of society. Both forms sustain each other; for psychoanalysis to be billed as an individual therapy promising health and adjustment, the critical and social components of the theory must be junked, since they plumb a social universe that precludes individual therapeutic claims to health. The preservation of such content — the metatheory of Freud — belonged to the very marrow of critical theory's reading of psychoanalysis; its preservation nourished the resistance to subjective notions of subjectivity, conformist in their capitulation to the immediacy of the subject's own perceptions. "Objective truth," is the "philosophical core of Freudianism." [80] Freud once affirmed, "The great ethical element in psychoanalytic work is truth and again truth." [81] He stated elsewhere, "Psychoanalysis demands a degree of honesty which is unusual and even impossible in der bürgerlichen Gesellschaft (bourgeois society)." [82]

This metatheory, psychoanalysis as an objective science of subjectivity, passes onto Marxism; negative psychoanalysis is psychoanalysis refracted through Marxism. This refraction calls for an examination of the individual — the object of psychoanalysis — in the light of developments since Freud's formulations. In brief, the transition to monopoly capital has dealt a mortal blow to the individual whose health was always ideology. "The category of the individual," wrote Horkheimer, "has not been able to withstand giant industry." [83] Psychoanalysis turns negative, a study of remnants; it explores a subject whose subjectivity is being administered out of existence.

The intent is to abet cracking the continuum of history. It pursues in the psychic dimension what Western Marxism has pursued in the nonpsychological dimension: the objective force of capitalist domination that has paralyzed the subject as an active historical force. The exact relationship between these two spheres is difficult to define. Negative psychoanalysis knows only a negative relationship; it examines the psychic forms that have diverted, impeded, or dissolved a historical and class consciousness.[84] It is tempting, and even partly correct, to draw exact parallels between these two dimensions; to transpose an analysis of reification as a form of consciousness to a psychic dimension, e.g., to find in the latter a frozen, rigid, nondynamic quality associated with the former. Marcuse himself speaks of the "reification of the ego," and studies of the "authoritarian personality" seemed to have confirmed its existence.

Yet the nonidentity between these two dimensions must not be forgotten, especially given recent developments. The psychic and character forms of reification are historically specific in a manner different from the nonpsychic; each has a different dynamic which is not insular but derived from the dynamic of capitalism. The concept of reification, as Adorno points out, must not be reified. It would be wrong to identify the sexually repressed, cold Puritan as *the* unchanging bourgeois character form of reification. Since Max Weber the spirit of capitalism, but not capitalism itself, has been redone. Today it is often the reverse: instant intimacy, smiles, liberation in one's own backyard.[85] Marcuse's concept of "repressive desublimation"[86] or Adorno's of "desexualization of sexuality"[87] are efforts to come to grips with the recent historical dynamic of the psychic dimension. This psychic dimension is as fluid and historically variable as capital itself; as the succession of capitalist forms accelerates, so do the psychic forms. In the blur, the dead shells of domination appear to come alive. Even the most resilient are turned into desperadoes hunting for pleasures in the amusement park of life. If critical theory as negative psychoanalysis is not to succumb to the lure of the chase nor flee into old slogans, it must plumb the psychic depths for sounds of sadness and revolt.

V

The Politics of Subjectivity

The political left has not escaped the ravages of social amnesia and subjective reductionism. The very effort to think through and back, which in different forms belongs to the best of psychoanalytic and Marxist thought, is undermined by the individual in crisis unable to think beyond itself. Evidence of this is everywhere, in revisionist and conformist psychology as well as in the left. The crisis is no fraud; the chill of social relations numbs the living. The effort to keep psychically warm, to stave off the cold that seeps in, shunts aside any time for or possibility of sustained thought and theory. The permanent emergency of the individual blocks the permanent and social solution.

Within the left this assumes a definite form. Because the political left is a left it retains a social analysis of society. The very problem, however, is that this social analysis decays more and more into slogans, thoughtless finds of the moment. The individual stripped of memory and mind magnetically attracts reified slogans that serve more to sort out one's friends and enemies than to figure out the structure of reality. This is a dynamic that keeps society rattling along; the very breathing space that could give life to critical theory is lost in the desperate search for life itself. The search without reflection grooves along in the ruts of society.

Social amnesia takes two forms within the left: the construction of instant and novel theories of reform and revolution, and, recently and increasingly, the hasty refurbishing of older slogans and tactics. Both proceed simultaneously because both live off the suppression of the past. The pop theories are fabricated out of scraps and

101

pieces of personal experience and the morning news. Jaded ones are picked out of left archives and, once cleansed of their historical context, content, and critique, are restored to service. These forms of social forgetting render a discussion of trends in the left doubly irrelevant; not only is such a discussion distant from the immediate needs of the individual, but it is obsolete, examining political thought and slogans that have already been discarded and forgotten. So rapidly does the left change that discussion and analysis seem doomed to lag behind.

Evidently this is part of the problem: attending to the emergency of the individual has absorbed sustained political energy and theory. The slogans that replace and dislodge theory shift with the moment. These shifts are not made through choice, discussion, and thought, but "automatically" — thoughtlessly and unconsciously. If the latest political opinions are improvements over former ones, it is not because the latter have been surpassed, but because they have been forgotten. They pass as they arose, uncritically, and promise to return. The hex that haunts left thought is the hex of bourgeois society: memoryless repetition. Thinking falls under the sway of fashion: change without change. If ideas such as "smash monogamy" are not promoted with the same vigor as previously this does not mean that they have been critically transcended, but simply that they have been dropped, to be elsewhere and later recycled and reused. Inasmuch as this discarding and forgetting is a continuing process, an examination of slogans, even if they are obsolete — which is by no means certain — may indicate forces that are hardly obsolete, that are as vital as society itself.

This analysis does not intend to simply equate developments within the left proper with those outside it, as if the two canceled each other out, confirming the wisdom that it is best to do nothing. That a political left and nonleft participate in the same drive toward subjectivity, that both suffer from social amnesia, is proof only of the virulence of society, not of the meaninglessness of political distinctions.

Further, it need hardly be said, the left itself is more and more fragmented; these thoughts are concerned with *trends* which tend to exert themselves, but are not evident everywhere. Such an analysis does not claim universal validity. It should be noted also that while it is impossible to discuss the left without drawing material from the women's movement, Weathermen, and so on, it would violate the very spirit and intent to read this as an indictment of specific groups. At best, one can say certain groups express with greater clarity trends that are present everywhere. But nothing more; neither that such developments are restricted to particular groups or, more erroneously, that these groups brought them about. Here, as elsewhere, the issue is society as a whole.

The rejection of theory and theorizing is grounded in the affirmation of subjectivity. Theory seems politically impotent and personally unreal and distant. Only human subjectivity — the personal life — is meaningful and concrete. The personal is said (or was said?) to be political, the political, personal. The identity of the two eliminates the need to pursue either separately. Theory and critical thought give way to human relations, feelings, and intuitions. The immediacy of these cuts to the quick of theory and thought: mediacy. The presence of the here and now in the form of subjective feelings banishes thoughts to afterthoughts and second thoughts. It instills an immediacy that stills reflection.

The promise held out by a focus on human subjectivity is lost if no attention is given to its place within society in general. Here the relation of phenomena within and outside a left is at once critical and fluid. For the cult of human subjectivity is not the negation of bourgeois society but its substance. Against a Marxist dogma that proscribed all subjectivity in the name of science, its articulation within the left was progress; but when this articulation becomes an exclusive pursuit it courts a regression that constitutes bourgeois society's own progress. The fetish of subjectivity and human relationships is progress in fetishism. The rejection of theory which seeks insight into objectivity in favor of subjective feelings reconstitutes a suspect Cartesian tradition in the reverse: I feel, therefore I am. The inner drive of bourgeois society was to throw the human subject back on itself. Descartes's thought illustrates this tendency. "My third maxim was to endeavor always to conquer myself rather than fortune, and to change my desires rather than the order of the world." [1] Human subjectivity was left to shift for itself: to examine and transform the self, not the universe of the self. To prescribe more subjectivity as aid to the damaged subject is to prescribe the illness for the cure.

The wholesale rejection of theory incurs the constitutional failing of the individual retailer; apparently free to buy and sell he is a victim of objective laws without knowing them. The private individual, free to pick and choose, was a fraud from the beginning; not only were the allotments already picked and chosen, but the contents of the choice followed the dictates of the social not the individual world. The "private interest is already a socially determined interest, which can be achieved only within the conditions laid down by society and with the means provided by society. . . . It is the interest of private persons; but its content, as well as the form and means of its realization, is given by social conditions independent of all." [2] Even as society announced it, the idea of the individual as an autonomous being was ideological. The unemployed, like the employed, were to think that their lack of luck, or their luck, was due to private abilities and was not determined by the social whole. No less are the private hopes, desires, and nightmares cued by public and social forces. The social does not "influence" the private; it dwells within it. "Above all we must avoid postulating 'Society' again

as an abstraction vis-à-vis the individual. The individual
is the social being." [3]

The fetish of human relations, responses, emotions,
perpetuates the myth; abstracted from the social whole
they appear as the individualized responses of free men
and women to particular situations and not, as they are,
the subhuman responses to a nonhuman world. As noted
previously, a rat psychology befits humans only when a
suffocating world has transformed men and women into
rats. The endless talk on human relations and responses is
utopian; it assumes what is obsolete or yet to be realized:
human relations. Today these relations are inhuman; they
partake more of rats than of humans, more of things than
of people. And not because of bad will but because of an
evil society. To forget this is to indulge in the ideology of
sensitivity groups that work to desensitize by cutting off
human relations from the social roots that have made them
brutal. More sensitivity today means revolution or madness. The rest is chatter.

The cult of subjectivity is a direct response to its
eclipse. As authentic human experience and relationships
disappear, they are invoked the more. Autobiographical
accounts replace analysis because autobiographies as the
history of a unique individual cease to exist. "To get in
touch with one's feelings" — a slogan picked up by parts
of the women's movement — hopes to affirm an individual
existence already suspect. Self and mutual affirmation and
confirmation work to revitalize experience denatured long
ago. Bewitched by the commodity, the individual turns
into one. The atomized particle called the individual gains
an afterlife as an advertisement for itself.

The exclusive pursuit of subjectivity insures its decline. Not against the drive of society but in tune with it,
it judges a social product to be a private woe or utopia.
What was exacted from the individual at the beginning of
its history — that the individual's freedom, labor, and so
on, were only subjective and personal — is promoted later

as its salvation. That parts of the women's movement have made subjectivity programmatic, repudiating all objective theoretical thought, indicates only the extent to which the revolt recapitulates the oppression: women, allegedly incapable of thought and systematic thinking but superior in sentiments and feelings, have repeated this in their very rebellion. Yet the point is not to resuscitate an official orthodoxy that eliminated any role for the subject. Critical theory and viable Marxist thought have worked precisely against this orthodoxy; it is a question of restoring a subject-object dialectic. The alternatives of pure subjectivity and pure objectivity are the alternatives of positivist thought itself. Marxist and critical thought must use another logic, dialectical logic.

The promise of radical subjectivity to escape political and personal irrelevancy is unfulfilled. While there was positive progress against an older, scientific Stalinist orthodoxy, it repeated in reverse the same sin: an indifference toward the content of bourgeois society that perpetuates this content. "The passage to theory-less praxis was motivated by the objective impotence of theory," wrote T. W. Adorno, "and multiplied that impotence by the isolation and fetishization of the subjective moment of the historical movement." [4] Subjectivity that forsakes sustained theory gravitates toward slogans that are not the crystallizations of discussion and thought but secretions of the existing society. As such they serve not to popularize thought, but to replace it. From "armed struggle" to "smash monogamy" they are not necessarily wrong in themselves, but wrong insofar as they are blank labels, indifferent, or rather antagonistic, toward content. They are to be applied anywhere and everywhere, as if indifference to concrete and definite conditions were the hallmark of revolutionary theory and not its negation.

Blindness to content is the social logic of a society that deals in exchange values: how much? No matter their tone, blank categories of affirmation (or condemnation) of armed struggle, the third world, leadership, men, and the rest, do not resist, but succumb to the inner mechanism of this society. The preservation of concrete dialectical analysis, even in idealistic form — to follow Lenin — makes intelligent idealism closer to dialectical materialism than vulgar materialism that is primitive and indifferent. The former, in its loyalty to the particular, preserves what a crude materialism, blind to distinctions, loses. What Lenin said of idealism can be said perhaps, for the same reason, of pacifism. Intelligent pacifism is closer to revolution than simplistic armed struggle.

The slogan of "smash monogamy" is of particular interest in elucidating the political content of a current slogan; to be examined is the extent to which such a slogan resists the drive of bourgeois society or, appearances notwithstanding, seconds it. From the start it suggests a violence that is hardly commensurate with its object, as if the forces out to sustain monogamy were to do so with cannon and gun. Rather to "smash" monogamy is to smash something unprotected, weak and frail, already despised and hated, openly or secretly. The open scorn and popular ridicule reveal the profound ambiguity of society toward its own product: maintaining marriage as a means of transmitting authority while suspecting it to be obsolete.

In fact, as discussed previously, the bourgeois family — and monogamy — as instruments of authority are being eclipsed by more efficient means: schools, television, etc. The father, as the wielder of the absolute power of condemnation or inheritance, is being phased out. The erosion of the economic content of the family unit ultimately saps its authoritarian structure in favor of complete fragmentation. Important in this context is that the family in its "classic" form was not merely a tool of society, but contained an antiauthoritarian moment. The family as an independent and (relatively) isolated unit preserved a "space" in which the individual could develop *against* the society; as a mediator of authority, and not merely an instrument of it, it resisted as well as complied. It supplied an intellectual, and sometimes physical, refuge which is the source of resistance. The notion — practically extinct? — that you can always come home indicates the protection offered against social domination. Within this space, the family relationships not only partook of the prevailing inhumanity, but also preserved the possibility of something else and better. "In contradiction to public life, in the family where the relations are not mediated through the market and the individuals do not confront each other as competitors, the possibility exists for men and women to act not merely as functions, but as individuals." [5] The use of "sisters and brothers" by the left itself recalls the solidarity that at least for a moment was nurtured in the family.

That the family — and monogamy — was a form of humanity as well as a form of inhumanity is crucial to the Marxist critique. To lose this dialectic is to invite regression; it means falling behind bourgeois monogamy, not realizing its human moment but eradicating it in favor of a new and repressive equality. It is this repressive equality that inspires and fuels the hatred and attack on monogamy, as well as that on privilege and exclusion in general. It belongs to the bourgeoisie's most progressive *and* regressive program: progressive in its democratic content against feudal privilege, and regressive in that it is ultimately grounded in the market of "equal" exchange and works to further the domain of the market. This equality is abstract, as money is abstract; knowing neither quality nor content, it registers only numbers. In its indifference toward the actual content of life, a critique sustained by equality signals its bourgeois ideal "that tolerates nothing qualitatively different." [6]

In different guises — always resisted by Marx — it emerged within and outside Marxism, as in critiques of wage-labor, classes, private property — and monogamy. Such critiques were directed against inequalities and sought only equalization or democratization. In recognizing only privilege and inequalities they worked to level — capitalism's own task. In losing the dialectical moment, they re-

gressed; not the abolition of classes but their equalization,[7] not the abolition of capitalist property but its democratization, not the abolition of wage-labor but its extension
to all, were programs based on a bourgeois ideal of equality.
Equality fixated on forms forgot the content that was inhuman, equal or not. A critique of capitalist property inspired solely by equality promises only an equality of
domination, not its end. Rather bourgeois property contains both human and inhuman moments, as does monogamy. Marcuse's essay on Marx's *Economic and Philosophic
Manuscripts* is emphatic on this: Marxism seeks the abolition of *alienated* labor and *class* property, not "labor" and
"property" which are the praxis of free men and women.[8]

It rejects both of the abstract alternatives that a critique founded on equality proposes: the abolition of all
property — primitive communism — or wage-labor for all
— utopia as a workgang. Rather, Marxism seeks to realize
the human and individual moment in labor and property
that goes beyond formal equality. Marx ridiculed those
who saw communism as the abolition or equalization of all
property. In his piece on the Commune, he wrote, "The
Commune, they explain, intends to abolish property, the
basis of all civilization! Yes, gentlemen, the Commune intended to abolish that class property.... It wanted to
make individual property a truth."[9] Or in the *Communist
Manifesto*: with the end of capitalism "personal property
is not thereby transformed into social property. It is only
the social character of the property that is changed. It
loses its class character."[10]

A passage in *The Economic and Philosophic Manuscripts* gives the fullest discussion of the communism that
does not transform capitalism, but by equalizing univer-
salizes it. To Marx it is no accident that the key to such
communism is its critique of bourgeois monogamy. The
passage is worth citing. Primitive communism:

> wants to destroy *everything* which is not capable of being
> possessed by all as *private property*. It wants to do away *by*

force with talent, etc. For it the sole purpose of life and existence is direct physical *possession*. The task of the *laborer* is not done away with, but extended to all men. . . . Finally this movement of opposing universal private property to private property finds expression in the animal form of opposing to *marriage* (certainly a *form* of *exclusive private property*) the *community of women,* in which a woman becomes a piece of *communal* and *common* property. It may be said that this idea of the *community of women* gives away the *secret* of this as yet completely crude and thoughtless communism. Just as a woman passes from marriage to general prostitution, so the entire world of wealth (that is, of man's objective substance) passes from the relationships of exclusive marriage with the owner of private property to a state of universal prostitution with the community. In negating the *personality* of man in every sphere, this type of communism is really nothing but the logical expression of private property. . . . General *envy* constituting itself as a power is the disguise in which *greed* re-establishes itself. . . . In the form of envy and the urge to reduce things to a common level . . . this . . . even constitute[s] the essence of competition. The crude communism is only the culmination of this envy and of this leveling-down proceeding.[11]

The full content of the regressive critique of capitalism is here articulated; founded on the bourgeois notion of equality, and partly driven by envy and resentment, it works to spread capitalism. Blind to content, it registers only privilege and exclusion and seeks formal equality. The denunciation — of leadership, theory, talent, relationships between two people or between a man and a woman as forms of exclusion and privilege — is part of this "crude and thoughtless" communism. Privilege seen only as a violation of equality is privilege seen through the eyes of the bourgeoisie. "The developed modern state is not based . . . on a society of privileges but on a society in which *privileges are abolished* and *dissolved*. . . . Free industry and free trade abolish privileged exclusivity ... and set man free from privilege.... They produce the universal struggle of man against man, individual against individual." [12] The logic of equality that sustains these critiques of exclusion and privilege is the logic of the market itself. It seeks to level — a utopia of complete pulverization of human relations and an interchangeability of individuals. The universalization of alienation, not its abolition, is its unconscious goal; it promises as liberation an equality of domination.

The point is not the mindless defense of monogamy, bourgeois property, leadership. Rather it is to understand their dialectical content which will make their abolition not regressive but progressive. It is to understand their human as well as inhuman content: monogamy not simply as mutual oppression, but as the attempt at a sustained relationship between two people; theory not simply as elitism, but as necessary insight into objective reality; leadership not simply as manipulation, but as a rational form of organization. The inability or refusal to grasp the dialectical content, as well as the open resentment, make talk about their abolition suspect; they express the desire to break down privilege and exclusion not so as to liberate but so as to share the spoils. The envy which would destroy in the name of freedom is too often apparent, e.g., communal groups which systematically set out to destroy exclusive relationships as threats to their own. The endless talk on human relations within the insular group works to promote group domination; it flushes out the last hiding place.

The critique of unique and exclusive relationships as crimes against democracy and equality has been formulated by bourgeois society's own advanced representatives, notably de Sade. The human individual — and body — is rendered totally functional, subject to all and everything. The progressive and regressive elements of bourgeois society have rarely been so clearly articulated: equality and democracy serve as a critique of privilege, to make way for mutual and equal domination. The indifference toward the actual human content of relationships makes de Sade's program at one with the bourgeoisie's own dream of liberation: liberation as a spree in the bargain-basement of human sexuality. In "Yet Another Effort, Frenchmen, If you would become Republicans," he proposed:

> Never may an act of possession be exercised upon a free being; the exclusive possession of a woman is no less unjust than the possession of slaves; all men are born free; all have equal rights: never should we lose sight of those principles; according to which never may there be granted to one sex the legitimate right to lay monopolizing hands upon the other, and never may one of these sexes or classes arbitrarily possess the other. . . . Love, which may be termed the *soul's madness,* is no more than a trifle by which . . . constancy may be justified: Love, satisfying two persons only, the beloved and the loving, cannot serve the happiness of others, and it is for the sake of the happiness of everyone, and not for egotistical and privileged happiness, that women have been given to us. All men therefore have an equal right of enjoyment of all women.

That this is not just an equality of women for men, but all for all is clear.

> If we admit . . . that all women ought to be subjugated to our desires we may certainly allow them ample satisfaction of theirs. . . . I would have them accorded the enjoyment of all sexes, and, as in the case of men, the enjoyment of all parts of the body; and under the special clause prescribing their surrender to all who desire them, there must be subjoined another guaranteeing them a similar freedom to enjoy all they deem worthy to satisfy them.[13]

This is the full content of the bourgeois equality and democracy unfolded: a utopia of total fragmentation and mutual exploitation. The rights championed are the rights of money that have been doled out to all; alienation is transcended by universalizing it. As such, these rights, like equality, are informed by the market — and forget the market; focusing on the abstract, they leave to one side the concrete economic content. "Right can never be higher than the economic structure of society." [14] The rights advanced of late by some on the left — rights of homosexuals, of control over one's body, and the like — participate in the same dialectic of bourgeois equality and rights; they are both progress in freedom and progress in domination. The right to free labor was the right to wage-slavery. The right to freedom of speech is the right to read a mass-produced newspaper. Their essential content was dictated by the economic-social structure of society, not by formal and abstract rights and equalities. And yet they were progress — against serf labor and state-run newspapers. So, too, with the newer rights championed.

This is not to argue that they are not worth struggling for; they are — just as wage-labor and freedom of speech were, and are. Yet not to be forgotten is the content; rights do not negate the prevailing society, but affirm and extend it. The right to "free" labor as that to free sex is ironic. It is the freedom of individuality which has already been killed in its substance. It is the gloss of freedom under conditions of its denial. When this content is ignored, then the relationship of these reforms and rights as part of a revolutionary process, but distinct from a revolution that would revolutionize the content itself, is mystified. Where these rights are announced as ends in themselves, the democratization of reification is dubbed its dissolution. The glorification of the rights of homosexuals, control over one's own body, group relations, masturbation, and the rest confuse equality-within-alienation with liberation. To romanticize masturbation is to hawk the quintessence of bourgeois society for its negation. The systematic destruction of human relationships has left the decimated subject only with itself. The concept of freedom lies elsewhere; it is anchored in the sustained relation between two individuals; it can transcend and go beyond this — and ultimately must — but cannot bypass it.

It was this moment which was saved in the Marxist "abolition" of bourgeois monogamy, and this is .why Marx and Engels spoke of monogamy as being realized, not obliterated.[15] The relation of two individuals, of loved and lover, belongs to the core of human freedom.[16] The positive content of this is unclear, as it must be till the liberated society has arrived.[17] Yet from Marx through Freud to the Surrealists and to the Frankfurt School, unique and individual love and relationships have been seen as elements of freedom, the rejection of a repressive civilization.

The drive to level, to reduce all to identical monads efficient and adept at shifting relationships with anyone or anything is the form of love of late capitalism. Unique love harbors a threat to this indifferent and collective form which is fabricated by bourgeois society or promoted by parts of the left. Eros is lethal for the repressive collective, and ultimately lethal for the lovers. The etymological link between (love) "potion" and "poison" indicates the psychological and historical one. Two people in love, by excluding the larger society, incite its wrath. "Two people coming together for the purpose of sexual satisfaction, insofar as they seek solitude are making a demonstration against the herd instinct, the group feeling," wrote Freud.[18] "The antithesis between civilization and sexuality," he wrote elsewhere, is derived "from the circumstances that sexual love is a relationship between two individuals in which a third can only be superfluous or disturbing, whereas civilization depends on relationships between a considerable number of individuals." [19] When human relations fall under the dictates of planned obsolescence, the unique relationship between two individuals smacks of freedom and resistance — and foolishness, exactly as foolish as repairing an old commodity when a new one is cheaper. According to Horkheimer, "Realistic science has objectified sex till it is manipulative. . . . In the mass society the sexes are leveled so that they both relate to their sex as a thing, which they control coldly and without illusion." Freedom is elsewhere. "The lovers are those who preserve and protect neither themselves nor the collective. In disregarding themselves, they earn its anger. Romeo and Juliet die against a society for that which it itself proclaims. Insofar as they unreasonably sacrifice themselves, they assert the freedom of the individual against the domination of property." [20]

If the intensification of subjectivity is a direct response to its actual decline, it ultimately works to accelerate the decline. To the damaged subject it proposes more of the same. The objective loss of human relationships and experience is eased by their endless pursuit. A cult of subjectivity — complete with drugs — dopes the discontented into taking their own death, figuratively and in fact, for life itself. The immediacy of it all drives out mediacy of any of it. Sustained political and theoretical thought is not simply rejected but forgotten and repressed. The slogans and rhetoric that replace it are as vacant and thoughtless as the society that tosses them up. The specter not only of society, but of its opposition, that has lost its memory and mind, haunts history.

The tone of the slogans notwithstanding, their collaboration with society is barely hidden. Empty concepts, too often fired by resentment and envy, perpetuate the essential content of this society. A critique of monogamy, theory, leadership, relationships between two people as forms of exclusion and privilege is a critique that falls behind bourgeois society, not advances over it; it is akin to the "thoughtless" communism outlined by Marx. What is perpetually lost under the sway of immediacy is a dialectical analysis: monogamy as both human and inhuman — as the bad refuge from a worse world and a bad solution for a better world; theory as insight into objectivity as well as elitism. To see only one moment is to trade the worse for the bad: no theory instead of elitist theory, inhuman fragmented relations for damaged human ones. The dialectical path is elsewhere.

The depletion of political concepts in favor of psychological and subjective ones is a by-product of the scramble for the remnants of human experience. Yet the subjectivization of objective concepts is not the repudiation of the loss of human experience but forms its prehistory. The reduction of the Marxist theory of alienation to a subjective condition by liberal sociologists has its counterpart in the left in the reduction of oppression to a whim of the individual. Alienation becomes a headache and oppression mere annoyance. "I'm oppressed," announces someone, and that's that.

Inside and outside the left radical subjectivity announces its own end; it resists reification by colluding with it. Hence the totalitarian urge of radical subjectivity to control everything. Endless talk about human relationships within the closed group promotes domination. Bad subjectivity seeks the bad collective that secures subjectivity by annihilating it. "Collectivism and individualism complete each other in the false." [21] The bourgeois individual whittled down to identical monads pursues its last fragments in and for a public only too anxious to share the remains. The individual goes public in a desperate attempt to maintain solvency. Blank and vacant affirmations or condemnations of the women's movement, men, armed struggle, recent political and personal events serve as tools of interpersonal relations. Thought is reduced to slogans and slogans to symbols of mutual- and self-confirmation.

Rampant narcissism surfaces as the final form of individualism; it at once negates the ego and perpetuates its mangled form. Vague conceptions of guilt, the universal oppression of women by men, one's "own" oppression, function as instruments of an ego that is regressing in the face of a disintegrating society. That men, too, have suffered and died in the massacre of history is affirmed or denied, but is in any case irrelevant. What counts is the immediate, and here an economism-turned-feminism is promoted as if the blind endorsement of what every worker did or thought is improved when it is as blindly applied to women. Social analysis decays into group loyalty. The jealousy with which the oppression of women, children, homosexuals, and so on, is defended as a private preserve, off-limits to others, expresses an urge to corner the market of oppression.

Again, the point here is not to argue for a return to a "scientific" objective theory that proscribed any role for the subject; and again, the alternatives of pure subjectivity and pure objectivity are the either/or of bourgeois culture itself. The choice between instant subjectivity and instant slogans, between unorthodox individual needs and political orthodoxy is no choice at all. Nor are the practical and communal attempts to overcome the deadly privacy and coldness of existence to be rejected. Rather they are to be advanced; but advanced not by a mode of thought and action that damns them to be more of the same. The political and personal praxis that is sustained by bad subjectivity and abstract slogans issues into the very prison that is the bourgeois world. What is to be sought is a concrete subject/object dialectic that reconstructs the new out of the decay; only the praxis that shuns the fetish can hope for liberation. There are no guarantees nor tried-and-tested methods. Mistakes have been and will be made; but the efforts must remain continually alive to the tension between the "personal" and the "political" without abdicating either or reducing one to the other.

The line that inspired the Weatherman name suggested one metaphor for the path of theory and praxis: you don't need a weatherman to know which way the wind is blowing. In classical Marxist theory this metaphor indicates opportunism, that is, subjectivism or the lack of principles; the willingness to swim with the current, be what it may. Obviously, Weatherman was a direct repudiation of social-democratic opportunism; not only by their actions and program, but also by their courage and dedication. And yet, as argued here, they as others unwittingly collapsed into a subjectivity and abstract sloganeering that is part and parcel of bourgeois society itself. The Lukács of *History and Class Consciousness* suggested another metaphor for revolutionary theory and praxis; he wrote there of the sailor. The sailor, like the weatherman, takes exact readings from the wind — but with a decisive difference: "without letting the wind determine his direction, on the contrary, he defies and exploits it so as to hold fast to his original course." [22]

VI

Theory and Therapy I: Freud

Not in any beyond, but here on earth
most men live in a hell: Schopenhauer
has seen that very well. My knowledge, my theories and my methods
have the goal of making men conscious of this hell so that they can free
themselves from it.

S. FREUD [1]

In the history of psychoanalysis, as in the history of Marxism, reformist practices threatened to supplant and suppress theory. Revisionism of both schools — psychoanalytic
and Marxist — crept toward a pragmatism impatient with
a nonutilitarian theory and reflection. As has been discussed, the most recent forms of revisionism are the by-
products of social amnesia and a cult of subjectivity,
themselves products of an administered society. In the
name of authenticity and progress, the very theory that
could comprehend both is phased out as dated and obsolete.

Without a critical theory, analyses — inside and outside a left — degenerate into common sense and prefabri-
cated slogans. The repression of theory in the name of
efficient practice takes its revenge by returning as malpractices: pseudo-therapy and phony revolution. Critical
theory resists pragmatic or Marxist calls for the instant
identity of theory and practice; this is to be quickly attained only by the suppression of theory. Rather, critical

119

theory seeks to preserve the contradiction of theory and practice by enunciating it. The relationship between theory and practice in general cannot be compressed into a single formula; it is a highly complex historical relationship. Theory is not to be reduced to practice nor cleanly severed from it. The identity of theory and practice is to be achieved in a nonantagonistic society; till then the relationship can only be one of conscious contradiction.

Within psychoanalysis, the same relationship of theory and practice is preserved, though in a different form. Psychoanalysis is a theory of society and civilization as a whole, as well as immediate practice, therapy for the individual. Marcuse subtitled *Eros and Civilization* "A Philosophical Inquiry into Freud" and wrote that the book is concerned with theory not therapy. "No therapeutic argument should hamper the development of a theoretical construction which aims, not at curing individual sickness, but at diagnosing the general disorder." [2] The most serious objection of the Frankfurt School to the neo-Freudians turned exactly on this point: they weakened the theory of psychoanalysis in favor of therapy.

Psychoanalysis as individual therapy necessarily participates *within* the realm of social unfreedom, while psychoanalysis as theory is free to transcend and criticize this same realm. To take up only the first moment, psychoanalysis as therapy, is to blunt psychoanalysis as a critique of civilization, turning it into an instrument of individual adjustment and resignation. The point is not to play one against the other; both theory and therapy exist within Freud in contradiction. The innovations and revisions necessary on therapeutic grounds are not identical with the imperatives of the theory. Changes in the former can proceed without changes in the latter because the locus in each case is different: one takes the individual as ill, the other civilization as ill. Measures taken to cure the individual are not identical with those taken to "cure" the civilization; to a point they diverge.

"The right to such reorientations in the interest of successful therapy and practice is not questioned here," Marcuse wrote of the neo-Freudians. "But the revisionists have converted the weakening of Freudian theory into a new theory." [3] This is what is crucial, that the contradiction between theory and therapy is lost, not that changes are made in the name of therapy.[4] Yet this is not to be misconstrued to indicate there is no relationship between the general theory and the individual therapy, and that theory ignores therapy.[5] Rather the relationship is dialectical. Individual therapy must necessarily forget the whole so as to aid its individual victim; how exactly it does this is *in part* irrelevant to theory. As Brown, whose discussion parallels Marcuse's, wrote, psychoanalytic therapy as a "technique . . . can be judged only pragmatically. Anything goes if it works." [6] This is not to be criticized — or if criticized, only when that which "works" is called liberation or growth. Theoretically, what Adorno wrote remains true: "In adjusting to the mad whole the cured patient becomes really sick." [7]

The acuteness of Freud as bourgeois thinker is here again glimpsed; he unflinchingly articulated contradictions and refrained from blurring them in the name of therapy or harmony. From his early writings to his last no attempt is made to reconcile individual therapy with the "meta-theory" of psychoanalysis; they exist in contradiction. Insofar as civilization was repression, individual therapy was education in repression, albeit conscious repression. Freud's concluding words from his first book, with Breuer, *Studies in Hysteria*, remain a scandal to therapists who would forget the theory so as to promote the therapy. Freud enunciated and distinguished these two moments. He cited the typical remarks of a patient who complains that

you say, yourself, that my suffering has probably much to do with my own relations and destinies. You cannot change any of that. In what manner, then, can you help me? To this I could always answer: "I do not doubt at all that it would be easier for fate than for me to remove your sufferings, but you will be convinced that much will be gained if we succeed in transforming your hysterical misery into everyday unhappiness." [8]

If the goal of "everyday unhappiness" is not one that today's therapists will inscribe on their banners, it is the unwavering appraisal of the real possibilities and limitations of individual therapy. So too would Freud in one of his last papers, "Analysis Terminable and Interminable," emphasize the minimal change that could be expected from therapy: "The difference between a person who has not and a person who has been analyzed is, after all, not so radical as we endeavor to make it and expect and assert that it will be." [9]

Freud was very much alive to the dangers of theory being absorbed by therapy. His terms were different, but the formulation was the same as Marcuse's critique of psychological revisionism; the immediacy of therapy or reforms rendered irrelevant a theory that promised nothing for the here and now but truth. The practical and immediate gains of therapy convinced the pragmatists that an unworkable theory was extraneous. Yet to Freud, as to those who resist revisionism within Marxism, theory is to be preserved for the very reason that the revisionists rejected it; because it is true and not because it is practical in the here and now. [10] *Psychoanalysis is a theory of an unfree society that necessitates psychoanalysis as a therapy.* To reduce the former to the latter is to gain the instrument at the expense of truth; psychoanalysis becomes merely medicine. "I did not want to commend it [psychoanalysis] to your interest as a method of treatment, but on account of the truths it contains. . . . As a method of treatment it is one among many." [11]

For exactly this reason Freud opposed the monopolization of psychoanalysis by medical doctors as degrading psychoanalysis to therapy. Almost forgotten is the vigor with which Freud defended lay analysis and, today per-

haps least known of his major works is his lucid and lively
Question of Lay Analysis. "We do not consider it at all
desirable for psychoanalysis to be swallowed up by medicine and to find its last resting place in a textbook of
psychiatry under the heading of 'Methods of Treatment.' " [12]
Freud honed the revolutionary edge of psychoanalysis; he
fought its professionalization and domestication. He wanted
to preserve psychoanalysis as a theory, not exclusively as
a trade. "I do not know if you have detected the secret link
between [*The Question of*] *Lay Analysis* and *The* [*Future
of an*] *Illusion,*" he wrote to Oskar Pfister. "In the former
I wish to protect analysis from the doctors and in the latter
from the priests. I should like to hand it over to a profession
which does not yet exist, a profession of *lay* curers of souls
who need not be doctors and should not be priests." [13] As he
stated, "I only want to feel assured the therapy will not
destroy the science." [14] Lay analysts are essential to psychoanalysis, Freud told Smiley Blanton, because "the psychiatrist who takes up psychoanalysis is interested in the therapeutic needs chiefly. This aim is not to be disparaged, but it is
not the main or even the essential aim of psychoanalysis. The
chief aim of psychoanalysis is to contribute to the science
of psychology and to the world of literature and life in general." [15]

It is not without interest that Freud foresaw that the
stripping of theory from psychoanalysis would be a particularly North American phenomenon; in this sense Freud
anticipated and feared the neo- and post-Freudians as his
successors and betrayers; and he correctly adjudged a cultural climate of optimism and utilitarianism that would
repress the discovery of repression.[16] Freud remarked to
Franz Alexander that under the pressure of success and
pragmatism he was afraid the Americans would turn psychoanalysis into a "watered-down eclectic kind of treatment procedure." [17] And he considered that Otto Rank's
shortened therapy was "designed to accelerate the tempo
of analytic therapy to suit the rush of American life." [18] He
wrote not long before his death that the fate of psycho-

analysis in America was that of a "handmaid" to American psychiatry; it did not develop into an independent autonomous discipline. This fate reminded him of "the parallelism in the fate of our Vienna ladies who by exile have been turned into housemaids serving in English households." [19]

If it would be wrong to state that Freud formulated the problem of theory and therapy just as critical theory does, so too would it be wrong to argue that he did not articulate the contradiction. Freud resisted the debasement of psychoanalysis to an instrument of medicine or pure therapy because he fathomed to what degree this entailed the subjugation of psychoanalysis to the given social order that it was to comprehend; reduced in this way, psychoanalysis loses its truth value. "My discoveries are not primarily a heal-all," he wrote to H. D. "My discoveries are a basis for a very grave philosophy." [20] "I have become a therapist against my will," he wrote to Wilhelm Fliess.[21] He told Abram Kardiner, "I am not basically interested in therapy." [22] And he remarked ironically, "We do analysis for two reasons: to understand the unconscious and to make a living." [23]

Freud continually rebuked what he called therapeutic optimism or enthusiasm.[24] This was a claim to cure, quickly and/or completely. If civilization was repressive and neurosis was deeply entangled in the unconscious, cures could only be protracted and partial. He wrote of Sandor Ferenczi, one of the first to depart from Freud in emphasizing the therapeutic potential of psychoanalysis, that "the need to cure and to help had become paramount in him. He had probably set himself aims which, with our therapeutic means, are altogether out of reach today." [25] "Out of reach" because the neurosis was informed by deep-seated psychological and social determinants that severely hampered any immediate cure. "The expectation that every neurotic phenomenon can be cured," he wrote, "may be derived from the laymen's belief that the neuroses are something quite unnecessary which have no right whatever to exist." [26]

The disjunction — between the immediate therapeutic possibilities of "happiness and health" and the repressive whole that precluded just such possibilities — is to be found even in Freud's least "social" writing, in his essays and remarks on psychoanalytical therapeutic technique. Here it is clear that Freud remained true to the metatheory and was continually alert to the social conditions that damned individual therapy to impotence. Even more; to the point that individual neurosis was a response to brutal social conditions, it is pointless for the doctor to aim to cure. The unresolved irony of psychoanalytic therapy within an unfree society is that it is possible only when it is impossible. "Psychoanalysis meets the optimum of favorable conditions where its practice is not needed, i.e., among the healthy." [27] To cure in an unhealthy surrounding entailed redoing the social reality. To refuse the latter was to refuse the former. Freud stated that the doctor must "occasionally take sides with the illness which he is attacking. It is not for him to confine himself in all situations in life to the part of fanatic about health; he knows that there is *other* misery in the world besides neurotic misery — real unavoidable suffering — that necessity may even demand of a man that he sacrifice his health to it." [28]

Freud took to task the attitude of "fanatic hygienists or therapists"; they forget the very necessity of neuroses. Neuroses possess "social justification." "And should one really require such sacrifices in order to exterminate the neuroses while the world is all the same full of other inextinguishable miseries?" [29] Especially within the poor classes, the neuroses contained a *raison d'être* — that of survival — that precluded curing without changing the social conditions. "It renders the sufferer too good service in the struggle for existence." [30]

For this reason there could be no real individual solution, only a social one. "In matters of prophylaxis ... the individual is almost helpless. The whole community must take an interest in the matter and give its assent to the construction of measures valid for all. ... There is a great deal which must be changed." [31] Nor is the class nature of existing psychoanalytic therapy veiled by Freud; we are but a "handful of people" whose work is restricted to the "well-to-do classes." Given the vast amount of neurotic misery "the quantity we can do away with is almost negligible." For this reason Freud backed the idea of state psychoanalytic clinics for the poor.[32] He stated at the anniversary of one psychoanalytic clinic, the Berlin Institute, that it made psychoanalytic therapy available to the "great multitude of people" who "suffer from neuroses no less than the rich." [33] In a letter of Freud to Putnam the dialectic of therapy and social change is fully articulated; therapy, utterly lucid as to its limit and strength within a repressive society, issues into a social critique and praxis of liberation. The importance of separating the two moments of psychoanalysis — as therapy and as theory — is here enunciated.

> I believe that your complaint that we are not able to compensate our neurotic patients for giving up their illness is quite justified. But it seems to me that this is not the fault of therapy but rather of social institutions. What would you have us do when a woman complains about her thwarted life, when, with youth gone, she notices that she has been deprived of the joy of loving for merely conventional reasons? She is quite right and we stand helpless before her. . . . But the *recognition of our therapeutic limitations reinforces our determination to change other social factors so that men and women shall no longer be forced into hopeless situations.*[34]

It was not lost to Freud that the impulse behind the innovations in "classical" therapy, the tendency to absorb theory by therapy, was a humanist one. Because Freud emphasized the protracted nature of therapy, the restricted range of applicability, and the minimal results — "everyday unhappiness" — the humanist response sought to abridge therapy, extend its applicability, and promise more. The differences surfaced most clearly in the question

of the analytic situation itself, where analyst and patient
met. The "classic" posture was that of "nonactivity" on
the part of the analyst; the analyst was not to act or react
to the patient with open love, warmth, affection, or other
emotions; if anything, the reverse. Freud recommended a
"coldness in feeling" and the model of the surgeon "who
puts aside all his own feelings, including that of human
sympathy." [35] He rejected the "expedient" of sham affection as an aid to therapy. "Psycho-analytic treatment is
founded on truthfulness. . . . It is dangerous to depart from
this sure foundation." [36] To the humanist innovators these
directions smacked of indifference and cynicism.

Ferenczi was one of the first to introduce activity and
affection into the analytic situation, which paralleled his
therapeutic optimism. It is not without reason that the
neo-Freudians have always been ardent defenders of Ferenczi, and have followed his lead in stressing the role of affection and love.[37] Clara Thompson, herself a neo-Freudian,
lists two contributions of Ferenczi: "The analytic situation
is a human situation in which two human beings attempt
a sincere relationship" and "One must give the patient the
love he needs." [38] As one enthusiastic partisan of Ferenczi
has written, "Psychoanalytic 'cure' is in direct proportion
to the cherishing love given by the psychoanalyst to the
patient." [39] Neo- and post-Freudians have made variants of
this their program. Fromm, in an essay from 1935, interpreted the difference between activity and non-activity
as that between warm affection and inhuman indifference.
He wrote that the contrast between Ferenczi and Freud
was one of principle. "The contradiction between a humane
philanthropic attitude that affirmed in an unrestricted
manner the happiness of the patient and a patriarchal
authoritarian attitude which was in essence misanthropic
'tolerance.' " [40]

Adorno refers to this type of criticism of Freud's coldness and inhumanity;[41] it assumes that love and happiness
are to be attained by their mere affirmation. Rather, Freud's
"coldness" does mankind more honor than a false warmth

that is to be turned on and off by command — snatches of the ideology of sensitivity. Freudian analysis is the steadfast penetration of the injured psyche. It takes so seriously the damage that it offers nothing for the immediate. If Freud mentions the surgeon as an analogue to the analyst, it is because neither promises that the internal wounds can be smiled away. The psychic surgery is not inhumane; rather it is a just appraisal of the damages wrought by inhumanity. The accent on the reverse — immediate warmth, emotions — threatens the indifference: the different wounds are covered by a blanket warmth for all. In a cold and cheerless world universal love and sensitivity is an impossibility; if it dared to be concrete it would quickly be exhausted. It is "sustained" only by ignoring the individual scars of its object: brutalized humanity. In fact, it seconds the damage by degenerating into a tool, an "art of loving," indifferent toward the object and applicable without distinction. Adorno likes to cite this sentence from *Civilization and Its Discontents:* "A love that does not discriminate seems to me to forfeit a part of its own value by doing an injustice to its object." [42]

Yet a love that does discriminate is no longer purely "subjective." To be sure, prevailing positivism renders the notion of objective analysis of love and happiness unthinkable; it decrees facts to be objective and shelves the leftovers as poetry. To critical theory, however, the notions of love and happiness are fragments of a social theory. Individual love, to be sure, must be subjective; but this is precisely the point. Today it is *objective* but billed as the reverse; it is prey, in form and content, to society. Again the dialectic: the subjectivity that parades its authenticity covers for a social reality that commands. For subjectivity to attain itself, to become subjective, it must achieve self-consciousness: insight into the objective reality that falsifies the subject. Without this consciousness, the subject is ideological, a tool of a repressive society.

This was exactly the drift of Adorno's critique of Kierkegaard's conception of love; Kierkegaard's inner and purely subjective love, indifferent toward the object, was conformist and ideological. The fetishized love reveals a cold and feelingless core: indifference toward the actual world. "This dialectic of love leads to lovelessness." [43] Eschewing insight into reality, love and sensitivity erode to the purely subjective, a blind and blank attitude. The coldness of warm, subjective love dwells in its refusal to glimpse the social mechanism that creates coldness. The obdurate clinging to subjective love drives it into its opposite, an apology for a loveless world.

Marcuse's thoughtful essay from the 1930s, "On Hedonism," pursues the contradiction. Happiness does not drop from the sky; it is grounded in personal needs which in turn are cut and shaped by extrapersonal realities and forces. The subjective happiness in its immediacy, the happiness that satisfies the individual, is already objective in that it does not arise from the deep recesses of the nonsocial individual, but from the entanglement of the individual with social structures and tensions. Happiness over a new car is happiness that has been drilled in, not spontaneously hatched. A subjective happiness that adamantly maintains its subjectivity is one of resignation; it takes the prevailing form of happiness as natural and human. "It accepts the wants and interests of individuals as simply given and as valuable in themselves. Yet these wants and interests themselves, and not merely their gratification, already contain the stunted growth, the repression, and the untruth with which men grow up in class society." [44]

An antinomy arises that is the misery of life in bourgeois society. A critique of the given and subjective needs and gratifications — a critique unveiling the degree to which they are social modes, unfree and unhappy — is one which exposes the social reality that blocks and mangles individual happiness. Yet in showing the distance between the prevailing subjective happy-unhappiness and happiness within, and identical to, freedom, it diminishes the present pleasures. Knowledge and happiness diverge in an unfree society. "Knowledge destroys proffered happiness. . . . Knowledge does not help him [the individual] attain happiness, yet without it he reverts to reified relationships. This is an inescapable dilemma. Enjoyment and truth, happiness and the essential relations of individuals are disjunctions." [45] This is a historical disjunction, not a natural one; it is the configuration of happiness and freedom in an unliberated society — a society in which the modes of happiness are unfree and the modes of freedom, unhappy. Today, one vies with the other; every solution is the wrong one.

VII

Theory and Therapy II: Laing and Cooper

No less than has the political left, the psychology of R. D. Laing and David Cooper and their coworkers has not been immune to subjective reductionism — a reductionism which in particular has lost the tension between theory and therapy. Again a preliminary problem: if it is unjust to discuss the political left as kindred to the nonpolitical conformist psychologies, it is equally unjust to include Laing and Cooper. The intent of their psychology is political and critical; the psychology of madness seeks to indict, not absolve, a maddening society. Their work seethes with discontent. In this as well as in their serious philosophical interests they radically diverge from the conformist psychologies.

Yet they do not escape the general fate. Though their thought genuinely resounds with political radicalism, revolutionary élan, and theoretical coherence; yet it finally dribbles into blind therapy and positivism, pop existentialism and mysticism. To the point that neither they nor their admirers appear to notice, it might not seem to matter. Yet it does matter. The critique of society is degraded to externals against the inner drift of their own work. Over time this inner logic takes its toll, on Laing and Cooper and on their followers. The critique, unable to sustain itself and hollowed of meaning, is a front for establishment psychology, political passivity, spiritualism, and so on.

The intention of the following is neither to sum up nor write off Laing and Cooper, but, hopefully, to be suggestive. Their work is itself unfinished, and it is uncertain

131

how they are to resolve the antinomies in which it is locked. Insofar as their work is incomplete, so too are these remarks. Finally, it should be emphasized that while no distinction is drawn here between Laing and Cooper, this does not mean that they are identical. Furthermore, attention will not be directed toward some of their coworkers, especially Aaron Esterson, who in some ways is closer to Laing than is Cooper. The justification for limiting this discussion to Laing and Cooper is found in their theoretical closeness, the relative abundance of their writings, and their general impact on a wide audience. As elsewhere in this book the critique does not claim universal truth, but neither does it seek to be simply defined by and restricted to the names under discussion; at issue are social and intellectual tendencies.

From the first Laing and Cooper have repudiated the regressive principle of the post-Freudians — that of the discontinuum between health and sickness — and in doing so have returned to a Freudian position: the essential unity of psychic phenomena. Yet this must be immediately qualified; in their most recent writings the disunity has been maintained in the reverse: the mad are sane and the sane, mad, and both are located in distinct camps. This in turn reformulates in reverse the bad identity of therapy and theory that is the mark of the post-Freudians. The latter naively identify individual and group therapy with social change. Laing and Cooper, on the other hand, openly in opposition to society, in flipping over the conventional designations of health and abnormality reproduce as a mirror image the same identification of therapy and social change. They tend to equate individual psychoses and madness with social liberation; they invest in the former what can only be reached by the latter. Hence, the noticeable glorification of schizophrenia, especially in *Politics of Experience*, as a "natural healing process," and "existential rebirth."

Laing and Cooper succumb to unresolved and unconscious contradiction which they do not, like Freud, articulate; [1] rather, in presenting them as transcended, they fall prey to them. We are told that schizophrenia is a "special strategy that a person invents in order to live in an unlivable situation." [2] Yet the content of this unlivable reality is whittled down to that of interpersonal relations, especially of the family; this was precisely the drift of the neo-Freudians: the social structure was adulterated to social friendship patterns. "There are no schizophrenics," Cooper tells us; and further, the conventional method of "abstraction" in which the schizophrenic is considered removed "from the system of relationships in which he is caught" distorts the problem. [3]

While there are sufficient statements designating the family as a mediating agency between society and the individual, in the main it is accepted as the cause of social oppression and not also its victim. The critique of the process of abstraction — considering the schizophrenic in isolation — issues into another abstraction: the family as an insular group. What Marcuse wrote of therapy among the neo-Freudians can be reformulated for this context. That the family is abstracted from society in the name of therapy aimed at a schizophrenic embedded in the family is not questioned; this is a pragmatic decision to be discussed among specialists, i.e., when or where individual or family therapy is more productive. It only becomes a question when this procedure of abstraction is promptly forgotten, and the family is considered society and not also its damaged product. When family therapy is billed as social change the imperatives for social change itself disappear.

An either/or is posed here which Laing and Cooper — and "radical" therapists — shy away from, but which is not arbitrary; rather it is rooted in the social structure. The social and radical analysis suggests that the individual designated mentally ill is ill not from personal defects; rather, the illness is a response to an "unlivable situation" that can be traced through the mediation of friends, family, jobs, and so on, to society. When one is loyal to this analysis, there can be no talk of therapy. More precisely: there can be talk of therapy, but therapy as therapy — not as radical therapy or social change. The therapy accepts for the sake of the individual victim the disjunction between the *individual form* of the illness and its *social origin*. In this way therapy becomes self-conscious, adequate to its own notion; it does not mystify itself as radical cure or liberation while it responds to the emergency of the individual victim.

But radical therapy is not loyal to the political and social analysis; it often confuses interpersonal, family, and social analysis. Out of the confusion emerge possibilities of therapy as "birth," "healing," "growth" that society precludes — if indeed society is even remembered. Rather, it is often forgotten by way of existential jargon, or it is spiritualized away by a new religious ethos. The former participates in all the difficulties of existential and humanist psychology, some of which were indicated above. With Cooper, especially in *The Death of the Family*, a radical, *individual*, existential standpoint coexists with an equally radical *communal* one. Commitment to oneself is as evenly accentuated as commitment to the community. Yet it is the very source of the evil that in bourgeois society the necessities of the individual and those of the collectivity diverge. To attain their identity in a free society presupposes the enunciation of their present antagonism. Cooper, however, unconscious of the contradiction, perpetuates it.

To follow him, insofar as the family violated the integrity of the individual, the duty of the individual is first toward him/her self. "The only way to compassionate involvement with others is the shortcut of one's own liberation," Cooper writes, as if this were not the very jingle that bourgeois society monotonously plays.[4] The shortcut of individual liberation cuts short the social liberation without which the individual is shunted into a dead-end street. Cooper relates an "existential" tale of a Japanese poet who chooses to pass by a small, desolate abandoned child because responsibility toward himself and his journey is of greater importance. The moral of this tale? "The hardest lesson of all is to know what one has to do for oneself." [5] Such is the blank existentialism that fantasizes it is negating bourgeois society even as it heeds its first precept: abandon the abandoned in the name of self-help first.

Yet this is not the whole of Cooper. Existential individualism vies with a communal and collective ethos. The contradiction is not merely Cooper's; it is one of an unfree society. The point is to find it and say it. To pretend that one is the other is to promote the myth that personal liberation is either personal or liberation. The only "shortcut" is via the detour of social and political praxis.

The thought of Laing and Cooper is nourished by various intellectual traditions of which two stand out: 1) a neopositivist social psychology and sociology focused on the group and group dynamics, and 2) a European philosophical existentialism centered on the concrete existing individual. While these two traditions may seem incompatible they converge in a single concern: the individual and his/her immediate context. In different language — "interpersonal perception," "intersubjectivity" — both traditions repudiate the study of the individual abstracted from the context of other human beings; both stress the network of concrete human relations. Both, however, ultimately work to eat away the social context of these human relations; they reduce social relations to immediate human ones.

The study of group dynamics within sociology or psychology is hardly new; it derives from an American as well as a German tradition, from Charles H. Cooley as well as from Georg Simmel and Kurt Lewin. Sociology itself has often been defined as the study of how social groups influence each other and their members. The attraction of this approach for establishment sociology is not difficult to discern; as Adorno and Horkheimer comment, the concept of society disappears to make way for endless empirical observations on group dynamics.[6] These empirical observations skirt the antagonistic relationship that is outside the laboratory — the individual and society — in favor of the safe, sound, and verifiable one of individual and individual.

With Laing and Cooper the group dynamic approach is extended to the study of schizophrenia. The promise is to understand schizophrenia by situating it in its immediate human context, usually the family. "Our interest," writes Laing (with Aaron Esterson) "is in persons always in relation either with us, or with each other, and always in the light of their group context, which in this work is primarily the family, but may include also the extra-familial personal network of a family." This method seeks to study "at one and the same time i) each person in the family; ii) the relations between persons in the family; iii) the family itself as a system." [7] The claim is that the "shift of view" from considering schizophrenia abstracted from a context to situating it within the family *"has an historical significance no less radical than the shift from a demonological to a clinical viewpoint three hundred years ago."* [8]

The shortcoming is that, from the standpoint of theory, society is shuffled out; the shift of viewpoints issues into the very problem of the study of group dynamics in general: a social constellation is banalized to an immediate human network. It is forgotten that the relationship between "you and me" or "you and the family" is not exhausted in the immediate: all of society seeps in. If it is clear that the immediate relationship of boss and worker, teacher and student, is grounded in a non-immediate social configuration, it is no less true of family relationships. Society as the determining structure dictates more than the husk of a relationship; it cuts into the living germ. Laing and Cooper are aware of this — but only aware. The awareness is not translated into theory, but remains on the level of continual observation.

The contradiction that inheres in all therapy turns into an antinomy. If the family is the immediate context of schizophrenia, it is not *the* context — society. Inasmuch as the limitations of family therapy are not acknowledged, the therapy begins to confuse itself with social change. Yet the very material itself, the case histories presented, shows to what degree the family, if it is the immediate situation for schizophrenia, is only one part of the whole situation. The question which is implicitly posed by the family analysis of the child schizophrenic is the origin of the parents that "caused" the schizophrenia. Evidently they emerged from other families, themselves caught in other networks, and so on; society enters by the back door. The family analysis pushes toward its limits. The facts discovered during the analysis, in suggesting that the family itself is victimized, confess that family therapy is insufficient. "Neither of Lucie's parents had emerged from their relations with their parents as persons in their own right. Both had been hopelessly immersed all their lives in phantasy unrecognized as such." [9] Or: "Mrs. Church herself had been subjected to her own four hundred blows, leaving her, as one report put it, an empty shell. Understandably, and indeed necessarily, Mrs. Church tended to destroy not only her own inner world but Claire's." [10] The "and indeed necessarily" captures the whole dynamic of society.

The problem is not that family analysis and therapy are being used; it is that therapy does not attain self-consciousness: lucidity as to its scope. Because the tension between family and society, theory and therapy dissipates, social theory and change are absorbed by family therapy. The unadmitted tension between the theory and therapy takes its revenge: the therapy, conceiving itself as dealing with the real context, inches out to include more and more people in this context and finally is damned to impotence, confronted by more people than any therapy could hope to "treat." Because the disjunction between society and family is neglected, the specific praxis suitable for each is rendered an amalgam suitable for neither. Laing cites with approval the therapeutic approach of a doctor whose "strategy was to reconvene the network out of which the mother had dropped in the past twenty years, eventually bringing together at one meeting upwards of thirty-five people, representing elements of no less than seven nuclear families. He did not 'treat' the son or the mother individually, or as a dyad, but 'treated' the whole network." [11]

The absurdity of this approach is based on the illusion that the therapist can "reconvene" the whole network of which the patient is a part, and secondly, even if it could be done, that these numbers of people could be "treated." The question, of course, is, why stop with thirty-five people, since they are evidently involved with another seventy, and so on. The implicit logic suggests the project of gathering all the members of society in one room, as if the antagonisms could be ironed out in the give and take of a group discussion. Objective conditions are refined into "bad vibes." At times, Laing has suggested that the entire world is an expanded family group, what he calls a "Total World System." [12] Truths adequate for family therapy degenerate into naive political pronouncements on "East-West relations" passed off as a family tiff. If there is a recognition of a distinction between family and society, the distinction is reduced to one of complexity, not of kind or structure. "New elements" and a "new gestalt" do enter into the "larger pattern"; with that proviso, "it seems that our scheme of the *dyadic spiral* for the interplay of true perspectives has relevance in the international sphere." The relevance is shown in the advice as to how to avoid an East-West conflagration. "If West thinks East thinks that West thinks that East thinks West is going to move first, the West" etc., etc. [13]

Forgotten is that society is not identical with a family, nor social relations with human relations; capitalism is not merely numbers of people involved in groups and families. A collaborator of Laing, Aaron Esterson, sums up the humanist reductionist principle thus: "A social system is simply the pattern of interaction and interexperience of the persons comprising it." [14] This is inexact. It is also a social construction and constriction which, if it is derived from human labor and activity, in turn dominates them; it is objective as well as subjective. A radical analysis of schizophrenia is committed to society as the determinant. Evidently the mediations are crucial, and the family is one of them. But they are mediations, not origins; the family does not exist in a no-man's-land. It is snarled in a historical dynamic; it has changed in the past, and it is changing now. It is as much victim as victimizer.

The reduction of a social configuration to a concrete and immediate one explains a striking feature and irony of much of the radical and existential psychology: the omission of a class analysis of mental illness. While there are unending comments and accusations that society is the villain, society is conceived either in immediate human terms or abstract universal ones — or both. In the former case, the agent of oppression is the family and network of friends, and this is interpreted as invariant throughout society. In the latter case, society is the direct cause, and is pictured as a universal and homogeneous substance. In both cases attention is deflected from decisive mediating agents such as social class. A vacant existentialism or a vapid social analysis blocks a finer investigation sensitive to class. The possibility and probability that certain kinds of mental illness are more prevalent in one class or stratum — or in families of that class — are ignored. The irony is that while the "radicals" have been indifferent, a class analysis of mental illness and of mental illness in the family forms a viable part of liberal social psychology.[15]

The point here is not to renounce family therapy or group therapy. It is to realize to what extent even the most extended therapy remains therapy: a choice in how to treat the individual that leaves untouched the social roots. In that sense there is no such activity as radical therapy — there is only therapy and radical politics. Need it be said? There is no shame in aiding the victims, the sick, the damaged, the down-and-out. If mental illness and treatment are class illness and treatment, there is much to be done within this reality. But the reformation of the social reality is another project, which if it is not utterly distinct from therapy, is not to be confused with it.

The question of the use of a medical or biological analogy in psychology can serve as a final clarification of the theory-therapy dialectic. Laing and Cooper, like many others, protest the use of such a model because it mystifies the social and human processes within psychology that are nonexistent in nonpsychological medicine. The very "diagnosis" and "definitions" in psychology enter into the dynamic of the situation differently than strict medical terms. For example, a medical diagnosis of tuberculosis, even an incorrect one, does not affect the disease, while one of "schizophrenia" may "cause" schizophrenia.[16] The definitions, the doctor, the immediate human context specify the milieu of psychology differently than in nonpsychological medicine.

This is undoubtedly true — but insufficient. The critique of a quasi-biological psychology in the name of society forgets that biological medicine is not outside the social dynamic. Clarity here could illuminate the theory-therapy relation that exists in *both* spheres: psychological and nonpsychological. The biological model contains a truth if it is freed from the mystification that removes it from history and society. The critique of the biological model lags behind a vast amount of critical literature that shows that not only medical care, but medical and "biological" diseases and disorders themselves are subject to a social dynamic of class, stratification, and so on.[17] If this be so, the theory-therapy dialectic can be pursued, as it is valid in both dimensions; without, however, losing all distinction between the psychological and the nonpsychological. Each dimension possesses a specific as well as a shared relationship to society.

The discussion (in Chapter III) of the social manufacture and perception of automobile accidents can be reconsidered in this context. Accidents are more than accidents. From the vast numbers of accidents "on the job" to occupational diseases, they are embedded in a social configuration.[18] So, too, with most diseases and sicknesses, from colds to infant mortality to malaria. None of these is randomly distributed in populations; they possess a social content. Chronic disease, for instance, is not a biological statement about the poor, it is a social statement.[19] The fact, however, of the social origin does not preclude treatment on an individual basis. The reverse is true: treatment on an individual basis must proceed at the same time that the theory suggests that the "ailment" and ultimately the "cure" is extra-individual. The victim of an automobile accident is not to be turned away by the politically aware doctor with the remark that he or she is not a victim of a specific car accident but a victim of an obsolete transportation system kept alive by the necessities of profit. Both are true, and both are to be preserved in contradiction. The emergency of the individual is to be attended to, even as it is traced to nonindividual and social factors which are the real source.

The situation of the doctor "treating" schizophrenia is in principle not dissimilar from that of the doctor treating black-lung diseases or automobile "accidents." While there is neither identity nor complete separation between the psychic and the somatic, the disjunction of theory and therapy is valid in both; the therapy in each leaves untouched the social roots — which does not mean that the therapy is unnecessary. The damage from "accidents," psychic and physical, needs to be healed. The battered driver is to be cured so as to return to the expressways, this time to die. Psychic transfusions are to be given to the schizophrenic so that he or she can be released into the madhouse called society. This contradiction is contained in therapy of each kind; it is to be elucidated, not veiled, as if some new treatment, be it for broken bones or broken souls, can magically escape from it. What Laing and

Cooper tend to forget is that if family and extrafamily therapy is progress over clinical therapy and analysis, this is progress in therapy, not in social theory or praxis.

The concentration on the family nexus that Laing and Cooper advocate entails a concentration in the dimension in which this operates: the present communicative inter- action of the family. The analysis proceeds on the plane of communication and the breakdown of communication, meta-communication and lack of communication ("spirals" of misunderstanding). The analysis uses terms such as "expectation," "validation," "confirmation," and "percep- tion" — terms which suggest communication in its verbal and nonverbal forms.

The drift of the analysis is not distinct from that of the neo- and post-Freudians; it ignores the psychic depths and the past for the present and accessible interhuman dynamics. It advances the same critique of psychoanalysis: psychoanalysis leaves out the social analysis. "Psycho- analytic theory has no constructs for the dyad as such, nor indeed for any social system generated by more than one person at a time. Psychoanalytic theory has, therefore, no way of placing the single person in any social context." [20] As with other Freud critiques already discussed here, the "social" that is then added is simultaneously flattened out, this time to become communication.

The weaknesses of the communication and interaction formulations are the weaknesses of common sense and Adlerian psychology: it is not that they are completely untrue, but that they are superficial. Further, they become the more untrue the more the surface analysis drives out the past and psychic dimensions. Increasingly this seems to happen. The family appears more and more as a power group, and schizophrenia simply a product of mismatched roles, expectations, messages, and so on. The family "in- vents" schizophrenia; or "schizophrenic symptoms are vir- tually whatever makes the family unbearably anxious about the tentatively independent behavior of one of its offspring." [21] Or schizophrenia is considered the product of preconceptions and expectations. Hence Laing suggests that an experiment in which a group of "schizophrenics" would be treated as sane and a group of "normals" treated as schizophrenic would show that expectation "causes" the disease. [22]

If in Freud neuroses and psychoses are rooted in an erotic and infantile past, and hence are completely or only partially eradicable, here they are dependent on the flow of communication. The communication models implicitly accept a parliamentary notion of reality where there arc no real antagonisms; in the official accounts all conflict and differences are traced to breakdowns in communication, as if real contradictions did not exist. The same notion is stated or implied by much of the communication theory of psychoses; repression and antagonism are sublimated to become mixed and confused messages. Hence, in Gregory Bateson, who pioneered this approach — and on whom Laing and Cooper draw — the ego-function is described as "the process of discriminating communicational modes." In schizophrenia "we must not look for some specific traumatic experience in the infantile etiology. . . . The specificity for which we search is to be at an abstract or formal level." [23]

Again: the point is not that these formulations are inaccurate, but that they are superficial. If within therapy a communicative approach is effective, this is not questioned. What is questioned is when an effective approach within the treatment makes claims to be more than a description of current processes. A breakdown of communication is more than a breakdown of communication; it is rooted in other tensions and antagonisms. Communication is a moment of existence, not the whole of it.

The confusion between the surface and the essence leads Laing and Cooper to make the elementary bourgeois error: they mistake the phenomenon specific to one historical era as universal and invariant. In brief, they take the human relations that prevail in late bourgeois society as human relations as such. In this they share the illusion of the role psychologies discussed in Chapter III; role behavior is passed off as human behavior and not as a degraded form of it. What Laing and Cooper barely broach is that the interpersonal relations that proceed exclusively in the track of images, confirmations, meta-confirmations, and so on, are already an alienated mode of behavior.[24] They represent the behavior and communication of the disintegrating ego.

When Laing writes that "human beings are constantly thinking about others and about what others are thinking about them, and what others think they are thinking about the others, and so on," [25] he neglects to add the crucial qualification: not all human beings, but human beings who have been mesmerized and mutilated. "Human beings" seek double and triple confirmation when the first fails; and the first fails when the ego that advances it fails. The ego, frightened over its own fragility, seeks endless confirmations it can neither give nor receive. The logic of human relations approaches the logic of paranoia: in every nook and cranny lurks danger. Confirmation hardly allays the fears; one needs meta-confirmation and meta-meta-confirmation. "What I think you think of me reverberates back to what I think of myself, and what I think of myself in turn affects the way I act toward you; this influences in turn how you feel about yourself and the way you act toward me, and so on." [26] "And so on": the task is endless, without escape or exit. In the prison of mirrors which is society, the lifers stare at the mirrors for signs of life.[27] Multiple reflections are the opium for the multiple wounds the ego has suffered.

This is not to argue that in a future and human society confirmations and meta-confirmations would not exist; they undoubtedly would. But they become an exclusive pastime in a society where the ego is profoundly injured. Total confirmation is an imperative where total insecurity is a reality. "Knots" become the norm of human discourse when the social noose is gagging the individual. This is the joyless reality — but it is also the façade: a façade because it is a reflection of an objective social reality that is hidden from view. The theory of interpersonal perception is a theory of the spectacle.

The effortless shift in Laing and Cooper from a stress on the real and interpersonal context of human relations to a symbolization of this context, from an existential reality to what sounds like a positivist one, which otherwise seems inexplicable, is due to their confusion of appearance and essence. Laing and Cooper, like role psychologists, are trapped in the façade which can be adequately presented but not comprehended by positivist logic. The maps and schemes capture the movement of reality, but only after this reality itself has reduced men and women to carriers of signs and symbols. The maps of human relations that they plot are the reified expression of reification: "p→(o→ (p→(o→p))) He thinks his wife thinks he supposes she loves him." [28] This is the loveless talk of a loveless reality.

The move from existentialism to positivism is eased by the façade which is simultaneously both: existential and positivist. What is meant by façade is not a false front for the real thing, but a façade in that the social and objective factors are veiled. Exactly because the façade *is* the immediate reality of human relations in modern society, in exploring it one can claim that one is exploring the existential reality; and exactly because this existential reality is alienated and dehumanized it can be adequately expressed in positivist schemes. Existentialism and positivism converge when the existential reality is a positivist one.[29]

In existentialism Laing and Cooper find their philosophical roots. "It is to the existential tradition, however, that I acknowledge my main intellectual indebtedness." [30] Also to be recalled is that probably the least read book of Laing and Cooper is *Reason and Violence,* an exposition of Sartre. A discussion of this matter is here impossible; in general the Sartrean existentialism as filtered through Laing and Cooper does not correct its original weaknesses — some of which Marcuse has indicated.[31]

One element of this existential tradition can clarify the subjective approach in Laing and Cooper that threatens to swallow the social and objective reality. Laing appeals to Feuerbach as the initiator of the existential discovery of the interpersonal reality. "Over a hundred years ago Feuerbach effected a pivotal step in philosophy. He discovered that philosophy had been exclusively orientated around 'I.' No one had realized that the 'you' is as primary as the I." "The presence of these others has a profound reactive effect on me.... Philosophically, the meaninglessness of the category 'I' without its complementary category of 'you,' first stated by Feuerbach, was developed by Martin Buber." [32]

Though anyone and everyone can and has been included in the grab bag of existentialism, the appeal to Feuerbach is not incorrect. But Laing and Cooper recapitulate not only the strengths of Feuerbach, but also his failings. His strength is that against the idealism of Hegel a human and materialistic reality is advanced. "Again and again Feuerbach insists that the starting point of philosophy cannot be philosophy but the actual life of man. The primary fact in the life of man is ... the existence of the human community." [33] But in Feuerbach the same antinomies surface as with Laing, Cooper, and humanist psychologists: the human community shrinks to the immediacy of the I/You encounter, and this is abstracted from the historical and social reality. History for Feuerbach and Feuerbachians turns into anthropology, an invariant. "The essence of man," wrote Feuerbach, "is contained only in the community and unity of man with man; it is a unity, however, which rests only in the reality of the distinction between I and thou." Or he wrote, "the true dialectic" is a "dialogue between I and thou." [34]

Marx and Engels took Feuerbach to task exactly for the reduction of a social reality to a timeless human encounter. Engels, in a fragment, ridiculed Feuerbach's I/ thou formulation. "Philosophy has reached a point when the trivial fact of the inevitability of intercourse between human beings — a fact without knowledge of which the second generation that ever existed would not have been produced, a fact already involved in the sexual difference — is presented by philosophy at the end of its entire development as the greatest result. And presented, moreover, in the mysterious form of the 'unity of I and you.'" [35] Or as Marx and Engels wrote in *The German Ideology*, Feuerbach "conceives of men not in their given social connection, not under their existing conditions of life, which have made them what they are; he never arrives at the really existing men, but stops at the abstraction 'man.'" [36] He leaves out the "ensemble of the social relations." [37]

To be more exact: what is lacking in Feuerbach is what is lacking in Laing and Cooper. According to Marx and Engels this is the conception of man as activity, as praxis. It is precisely for this reason that Marx, to follow Marcuse, "reaches back beyond Feuerbach to Hegel." [38] For Hegel the concept of labor is the irreplaceable element of human history. Here labor does not merely mean factory work; it means the life praxis of man — objectification in the social world. Labor is the specific mode of activity for human existence; alienated labor is one form of labor, not labor itself.[39]

Because objectification or praxis is lacking in Feuerbach, his theory, for all its humanism, its I/thou, is a passive one. It does not comprehend the world as a social environment, the congealed product of human praxis. This failure Laing and Cooper share with Feuerbach; they succumb to the spectacle: the nonactivity of watching and viewing and being watched. What Marcuse wrote of Feuerbach could be written of Laing and Cooper. "In Feuerbach man's possession of, and relation to, the world remains essentially theoretical, and this is expressed in the fact that the way of relating ... is 'perception.' In Marx, to put it briefly, labour replaces this perception, although the central importance of the theoretical relationship does not disappear; it is combined with labour in a relationship of dialectical interpenetration." [40]

The logic of Laing and Cooper's approach to human relations is Feuerbachian; interpersonal perceptions, images, expectations constitute the fundamental determining structure; they are in no way secondary. In Laing and Cooper they dislodge the basic mode of appropriation of the world, human praxis. "Self-identity," writes Laing, "is constituted not only by our looking at ourselves, but also by our looking at others looking at us. . . . At this more complex, more concrete level, self-identity is a synthesis of my looking at me with my view of others view of me." [41] This is the theory of the spectacle; the passivity of the consumer is elevated into a theory of human identity.[42] Because the means of production and reproduction of life are agents of lifeless capital and profit, life itself seeks refuge in nonactivity; human praxis in this world contracts to you watching me watching you watching me. Passive watching is the sanctioned form of relief in a society that has squeezed out the only relief: active human experience. The peep show is no longer the side show but, with audience participation, is society itself. Laing and Cooper elaborate this into a theory of human — not inhuman — relations.

Finally: as existence turns into positivism (the reign of things over life) nondialectical logic knows only one escape: mysticism, spiritualism, and the like. This is an emphatic note in Laing and Cooper; today it is part of the *Zeitgeist*. The prevailing forms of reason and reality are confused with reason itself, and it is supposed that the nonrational is an alternative outside of present reality and in fact not further in it. The assumption that mystification is a response to alienation, "inner" space to the lack of "outer" space, was advanced long ago and has gained nothing in the interim.

The key to the logic is crystallized in the debate between Marcuse and Norman O. Brown about the latter's *Love's Body*. Brown wrote in a rebuttal to Marcuse's re-

view, "The alternative to reification is mystification." [43]
This is the crux of the matter. To critical theory, mystification is the complement to reification, not its dissolution.
It seeks to trick away reification by using reification's own
tricks: to make things dance before the eyes while society
limps along. If "our time has been distinguished ... by an
almost total forgetfulness of the internal world," to follow
Laing, it is not to be called to life by forgetting the outer
world that forgot the inner one. The promise of the "universal unleashing of a full spirituality" (Cooper) will turn
into a universally controlled and programmed reality if it
is not translated into social praxis. "Occultism," wrote
Adorno, "is the complement of reification. When the objective world appears to the living as blinder than ever before
they attempt to find meaning in it by abracadabra." [44] '

Today, half-serious mystics vie with totally serious
ones; stars, signs, gurus interpret a world of capitalist
hieroglyphics. The messages from the stars inadvertently
tell the truth: the daily fate and plight is irrational — it is
in the stars. [45] Hence it soothes those who suspect that life
is as predetermined as it actually is by shifting the blame
from the social to natural and supernatural reality. But
today the cults are a response not only to a cold and bleak
society, but to a political and cultural left that promised
too much too fast. Those who banked everything on a revolution "now" were left with nothing when the time schedule
changed. A "law" to be formulated? Mystical politics
produces mysticism without politics. The very recent in-
terviews with Laing suggest this progression.

Not to be forgotten is the strength of the writing of
Laing and Cooper. In a period when reason is mad, madness has its reason. Laing, Cooper, and their collaborators
have emphasized this insight. But as has been argued here,
this has more and more eroded into a parenthesis in a text
of pop existentialism, positivism, and spiritualism. The
text itself loses the tension between theory and therapy,
and advances notions of human identity and relations that
take the mutilated wrecks that people the social landscape

as specimens of a future humanity. Endless talk on I and thou forgets that neither can be created out of endless talk. The writings of Laing and Cooper more and more suggest the confusion of psychic first aid with liberation.

*   *   *

To read successively Freud, the neo-Freudians, and the post-Freudians is to witness the effect of social amnesia: the repression of critical thought. The vital relationship between mind and memory turns malignant; oblivion and novelty feed off each other and flourish. Psychoanalytic and critical thought is sloughed off in the name of progress which is regression. What has been called the "death and rebirth of psychology," referring to the reemergence of a spiritualized psychology since the demise of the "old" Freudian materialism,[46] is exactly the reverse: the loss of a critical psychology. The spiritualities of the conformists, the blind materialism of the behaviorists, the superficial humanism and confused existentialism, the rampant subjectivism: these are elements of a consciousness that no longer coheres. In this situation critical theory is loyal to its content: critique and theory, negative psychoanalysis and a nonsubjective theory of subjectivity. It resists the lure of the immediate which becomes irresistible as society hardens and rigidifies; and it works to preserve its alienation from an alienated society. "Nur Fremdheit ist das Gegengift gegen Entfremdung," wrote Adorno.[47] "Only distance is the antidote to estrangement."

The whole is the truth; and the whole is false. These are not mere theoretical statements, derived from Marx and Hegel. The madness and irrationality of the whole are so apparent, so evident, and so total that those who glimpse its full unreason are struck dumb by it. Their failing is not to understand what is not to be understood. It is left to the others to talk for them. No one is immune. Madness haunts the working and sleeping hours of even the most "healthy" and "normal" as society loses even the appearance of rationality. Liberation is so close that it can almost be tasted; and it is no longer comprehensible why it is not here. Those who repress this evoke the discipline and values of the past — the values that form the prehistory of the crisis, not its negation. Those who sense the nearness and distance of liberation tolerate the contradiction only with the greatest strain. Especially in periods of political retreat they are threatened with despair and resignation.

A critical psychology must not succumb; it must not forget the madness of the whole and ideologically flaunt the virtues of a human existence that is today inhuman. It must aid the victims — the lost, the beaten, the hopeless — without glorifying them. Shortly before the apparatus of Law and Order unleashed its bullets on the inmates and guards at Attica State Prison a prisoner was reported as saying: we are the only civilized men here. A psychology that is to be neither the cynical tool of adjustment nor the sincere but vacuous exponent of growth and sensitivity must reflect on that statement.

Notes

Introduction

1. William L. Langer's essay was given as a presidential address to the American Historical Association in 1957 and subsequently published in the *American Historical Review* under the title, "The Next Assignment." Preserved Smith's study, "Luther's Early Development in the Light of Psychoanalysis," appeared in the *American Journal of Psychology* (July 1913), pp. 360–77.
2. Erik H. Erikson, *Young Man Luther* (New York, 1958), p. 28.
3. What Norman O. Brown says in connection with this observation is directly relevant to the preceding discussion about the uses of psychoanalysis for historians. Noting that Freud "postulated a far-reaching but mysterious connection between the human body and human character and ideology" but found it difficult to specify the exact nature of the connection, Brown goes on to observe that the neo-Freudians, on the other hand, "opened the door to historical considerations," at the expense, however, of everything that was original and penetrating in psychoanalytic theory. "They thus return to what are essentially pre-Freudian categories of man and history, decorated with unessential (and confusing) psychologistic patter."

   Brown continues: "At the abstract theoretical level, psychoanalytical paradox and historical common sense are so far apart that one can only despair of ever unifying them. It therefore seems inevitable that progress will be made, if at all, by concrete empirical investigation. And since in general psychoanalytical considerations grope so far beneath the surface that they can easily be dismissed as arbitrary constructions not based on facts, such concrete empirical investigations must take as their point of departure, not psychoanalytical imputations as to what may (or may not) be going on in the Unconscious, but historical fact" — such as the fact of Luther's revelation on the privy.

"In my profession," Erikson writes, "one learns to listen to exactly what people are saying" (*Young Man Luther,* p. 64). This may be the most important thing historians can learn from psychoanalysis — not that ideas are rooted in a "pathological feeling of guilt."

4. It is not only those trained as historians, of course, who take what purports to be a historical approach to Freud. The neo-Freudian strategy from the beginning was to show that "Freud was in many respects limited by the thinking of his time, as even a genius must be" (Clara Thompson, *Psychoanalysis: Evolution and Development* [New York, 1950], p. 132). More recently such arguments have been taken up by feminists; see, for example, Ronald V. Sampson, *The Psychology of Power* (New York, 1966), pp. 45 ff.; Eva Figes, *Patriarchal Attitudes* (New York, 1970), etc. Even when historians have had no interest in the polemical issues that thus almost inevitably surround the historicization of Freud, their own bias as historians leads them to take such an approach. See, for example, H. Stuart Hughes, *Consciousness and Society* (New York, 1958), p. 126: "However much Freud's thought strove to be universal in its range, it was obviously bound by its creator's own mental endowment and early experience." Recently Carl Schorske has undertaken a historical and biographical interpretation of Freud's concepts (*American Historical Review,* 1973). In what follows I am concerned with "historical" interpretations of psychoanalysis in general, not merely with the work of historians.

As Jacoby shows, Freud himself was well aware of the way in which these interpretations — later presented as a dazzling new way of approaching the subject — were used to discredit his work. "This theory," he wrote in *The History of the Psychoanalytic Movement* — the theory, that is, that psychoanalysis was rooted in Viennese culture — "always seems to me quite exceptionally stupid."

5. Incidentally, the historicization of Freud ironically obscures precisely what is historical in his thought. "Psychoanalysis is the most radically historical psychology: this is its basic challenge to all other psychologies, and it is only in terms of this challenge that historians can finally evaluate its usefulness to them. In liberating themselves from grossly nonhistorical principles of ex-

planation — gods and demons, dialectical materialisms and idealisms, etc. — historians have come to see their task as that of understanding the interactions between the human agents of history with their environment. But this has not safeguarded them from neglecting their main task: to incorporate those human agents themselves fully into history. Freud made the most radical effort to explain the existence of these agents — 'mind,' 'spirit,' 'soul,' 'instincts,' the 'individual,' the 'self,' 'human nature' itself — in exclusively historical terms. The alternative to an historical psychology must be at some point simply to postulate the existence of something standard, normal and even normative that 'behaves' in history, and to do this, simply to postulate it, is to surrender the historical method" (Donald Meyer, review of Erikson's *Young Man Luther*, in *History and Theory*, I, 3, p. 294).

6. To be sure, the origins of the "revolt against positivism" go back to the late nineteenth century. Jacoby's formulation of the issues, however, seems to me more useful than that of Hughes (above, note 4), who overlooks the importance of the revival of dialectical traditions as an element in the revolt against positivism and who, on the other hand, exaggerates the importance of irrationalism as a pervasive feature of the cultural milieu at the end of the nineteenth century. Eager to show that thought is rooted in the *Zeitgeist*, Hughes's treatment is open to the objection that the best thought of any age attempts precisely to transcend the cultural milieu.

7. Theories of American exceptionalism had certain tactical advantages, to be sure, when it was a matter of resisting dogmatic demands for the Bolshevization of the American socialist movement — themselves based on a refusal to recognize that the revolutionary wave had receded, perhaps for good. Thus the Debsian socialists were able to argue (unsuccessfully, as it turned out) that purging the movement of social democrats on the grounds that the social democrats had supported the war made little sense in a country where the Socialist party had opposed the war. The Debsian socialists also understood that the revolutionary crisis had passed and that the strategy of Bolshevization, which was based on the assumption of its continuation, was based on a misreading of recent events (see James Weinstein, *The Decline of American Socialism* [New York, 1967], and my *Agony of the American Left* [New York, 1969]). But this understanding of the tactical and strategic implications of the passing of the revolu-

tionary crisis in Western society was not accompanied, unfortunately, by an understanding of its theoretical implications.

8. Theodor W. Adorno, "Scientific Experiences of a European Scholar in America," in *The Intellectual Migration,* eds. Donald Fleming and Bernard Bailyn (Cambridge, Massachusetts, 1969), p. 357.

9. See the attack on Marcuse's aloofness and "remoteness" by Ronald Aronson, "Dear Herbert," in *The Revival of American Socialism,* ed. George Fischer (New York, 1971), pp. 257–80.

Preface

1. The small scandal that Marcuse's essay "Repressive Tolerance" (in *A Critique of Pure Tolerance* [Boston, 1965]) caused is itself illustrative of how much has been forgotten. "Toleration is not the *opposite* of Intolerance, but is the *counterfeit* of it. Both are despotisms. The one assumes to itself the rights of withholding Liberty of Conscience, and the other of granting it." This is not Marcuse but Thomas Paine in 1791, in the *Rights of Man,* ed. Henry Collins (Middlesex, England, 1969), p. 107.

2. Sigmund Freud, *New Introductory Lectures* (New York, 1964), p. 160.

3. See Theodor W. Adorno, "Spätkapitalismus oder Industriegesellschaft?" in his *Aufsätze zur Gesellschaftstheorie* (Frankfurt, 1970), pp. 149 ff. Cf. Robin Blackburn, "The New Capitalism," in *Ideology in Social Science,* ed. R. Blackburn (New York, 1973), pp. 164 ff.

4. For a survey of Frankfurt School thought and history see Martin Jay, *The Dialectical Imagination: A History of the Frankfurt School and the Institute of Social Research* (Boston, 1973); and for a critical discussion of Jay's book see my "Marxism and the Critical School" in *Theory and Society,* I, 2 (1974), pp. 231 ff.

5. Harry Guntrip, a partisan of the object-relations theory, in his *Psychoanalytic Theory, Therapy, and the Self* (New York, 1973), demonstrates a kinship between the two schools — a kinship which extends to sharing the weaknesses of the neo-Freudians.

I   Social Amnesia and the New Ideologues

1. "Freud was, in short, heir to all the sexual mythology of his age" (*Masculine/Feminine,* eds. Betty and Theodore Roszak [New

York, 1969], p. 20). "Freud [was] beyond question the strongest individual counterrevolutionary force in the ideology of sexual politics during the period" (Kate Millett, *Sexual Politics* [Garden City, N.Y., 1970], p. 178). Such statements, if excusable because of Freud's writings on women, pass to the inexcusable. "Sexuality was a great threat to Freud. . . . He demanded authoritarian social control to guarantee the success of familial sexual repression on a widespread societal scale. In 1933 his wish came true, but the Nazis were ungrateful and Freud was disappointed" (Phil Brown, "Civilization and Its Dispossessed," in *Radical Psychology*, ed. P. Brown [New York, 1973], p. 246). As has been justly observed, "That Freud, personally, had a reactionary ideological attitude toward women in no way affects his science. . . . That he partook of the social mores and ideology of his time whilst he developed a science that could overthrow them is neither a contradiction nor a limitation of his work" (Juliet Mitchell, *Woman's Estate* [Middlesex, England, 1971], p. 167).

2. Karen Horney, *New Ways in Psychoanalysis* (New York, 1966), p. 37.

3. Clara Thompson, *Psychoanalysis: Evolution and Development* (New York, 1957), p. 132.

4. Patrick Mullahy, *Oedipus: Myth and Complex* (New York, 1955), pp. 316, 320.

5. Betty Friedan, *The Feminine Mystique* (New York, 1964), p. 97.

6. Sigmund Freud, "On the History of the Psychoanalytic Movement," *Collected Papers* (London, 1957), vol. 1, p. 325. After my book was completed and readied for publication Juliet Mitchell's *Psychoanalysis and Feminism* (New York, 1974) appeared. A discussion of her book, which in some ways shares the approach of mine, is impossible here. Only to be noted is that she makes a similar — and more extensive — response to the charge that Freud was intellectually bound and stunted by a nineteenth-century Vienna; see especially pp. 319 ff. and 419 ff.

7. Joseph Wortis, *Fragments of an Analysis with Freud* (New York, 1954), p. 142.

8. Wilhelm Lunen, "The Problem of Social Consciousness in Our Time," *Contemporary Issues*, 8, no. 32 (1957), p. 480.

9. Max Horkheimer and Theodor W. Adorno, *Dialektik der Aufklärung* (Amsterdam, 1947), p. 274. Unfortunately this is mistranslated in the English edition. "Alle Verdinglichung ist ein

158   *Notes*

Vergessen" is rendered "All objectification is a forgetting" (*Dialectic of Enlightenment* [New York, 1972], p. 230). To lose the distinction between objectification and reification is to lose the distinction between Hegel and Marx. Also, Ernest G. Schachtel's essay on amnesia remains well worth consulting ("On Memory and Childhood Amnesia" in *A Study of Interpersonal Relations*, ed. Patrick Mullahy [New York, 1957], and in Ernest Schachtel, *Metamorphosis* [London, 1963]).

10. Karl Marx, *Resultate des unmittelbaren Produktionsprozesses* (Frankfurt, 1970), pp. 17–18. Throughout this book where no English source is given, the translation is my own.
11. Daniel Bell, *The End of Ideology* (New York, 1962), pp. 404, 402.
12. Hannah Arendt, *The Origins of Totalitarianism* (Cleveland, New York, 1958), p. 468.
13. *Ibid.*, p. 458.
14. See George Lichtheim's essay "The Concept of Ideology," in *Studies in the Philosophy of History*, ed. George H. Nadel (New York, 1965).
15. See "Ideology" in Frankfurt Institute for Social Research, *Aspects of Sociology* (Boston, 1972), pp. 182 ff. and in Institut für Sozialforschung, *Soziologische Exkurse* (Frankfurt, 1956), pp. 162 ff. Mannheim's *Ideology and Utopia* is the crucial work in the domestication of the Marxist concept. Lichtheim calls it "the positivist's rejoinder" to Lukács's *History and Class Consciousness*. The Frankfurt School critically appraised it soon after it appeared. See Max Horkheimer, "Ein neuer Ideologiebegriff?" (1930) reprinted in *Ideologie*, ed. K. Lenk (Neuwied, 1964) and Herbert Marcuse, "Zur Wahrheitsproblematik der soziologischen Methode," *Die Gesellschaft*, VI (1929), pp. 356 ff.
16. Cited in Horkheimer and Adorno, *Dialectic of Enlightenment*, p. 41.
17. A portion of these remarks on Roszak appeared in Russell Jacoby, "Marcuse and the New Academics," *Telos*, 5 (1970), pp. 188 ff.
18. Theodore Roszak, *The Making of a Counter Culture* (Garden City, 1969), pp. 84 ff.
19. For a critique of Bell's and Robert Tucker's dubious interpretations of Marx and alienation, see István Mészáros, *Marx's Theory of Alienation* (London, 1970), pp. 227 ff., 331 ff. For a discussion of the various positions on the early and late Marx, see

Ernest Mandel, *The Formation of the Economic Thought of Karl Marx* (New York, 1971), pp. 154 ff.

20. "Not the last task that is set before thought is to turn all reactionary arguments against Western culture into service of progressive enlightenment" (Adorno, *Minima Moralia* [Frankfurt, 1964], p. 254). A fine example of this kind of work is Raymond Williams's *Culture and Society* (Garden City, 1960).

21. Erich Fromm, "Psychoanalysis — Science or Party-Line?" in *The Dogma of Christ* (New York, 1963), pp. 131 ff.

22. Cited in Carl M. and Sylvia Grossman, *The Wild Analyst: The Life and Work of Georg Groddeck* (New York, 1965), p. 113.

23. Rosa Luxemburg, "Reform or Revolution," in *Rosa Luxemburg Speaks,* ed. Mary-Alice Waters (New York, 1970), p. 87.

24. "The assumption that there are unconscious mental processes, the recognition of the theory of resistance and repression, the appreciation of the importance of sexuality and of the Oedipus Complex — these constitute the principal subject-matter of psychoanalysis and the foundations of its theory" (Sigmund Freud, "Two Encyclopedia Articles," *Collected Papers* [London, 1957], vol. 5, p. 122).

25. Herbert Marcuse, *Eros and Civilization* (New York, 1962), p. 11.

26. Norman O. Brown, *Life Against Death* (New York, 1959), p. 3.

27. Fromm, "The Human Implications of Instinctivistic 'Radicalism,'" *Dissent,* II, 4 (1955), p. 349.

28. Fromm, *The Revolution of Hope* (New York, 1968), p. 9.

29. Cited in Lelio Basso, "Rosa Luxemburg: The Dialectic Method," *International Socialist Journal,* III, 16–17 (1966), p. 518.

30. Fromm, *The Revolution of Hope,* pp. 143, 157.

31. Marcuse, "A Reply to Erich Fromm," *Dissent,* III, 1 (1956), p. 81.

32. See Loren Baritz, *Servants of Power* (New York, 1965), and Georges Friedmann, *Industrial Society* (New York, 1964).

33. Hugo Münsterberg, *Psychology and Industrial Efficiency* (Boston, 1913), pp. 50–51.

34. Cited in Reinhard Bendix, *Work and Authority in Industry* (New York, 1963), pp. 287–88.

35. Kenneth Benne, "History of the T-Group in the Laboratory Setting," in *T-Group Theory and Laboratory Method,* ed. Leland P. Bradford et al. (New York, 1964), pp. 86, 91.

II Revisionism: The Repression of a Theory

1. Ernst L. Freud, ed., *Letters of Sigmund Freud and Arnold Zweig* (New York, 1970), p. 59.
2. Alfred Adler, *The Science of Living*, ed. Heinz L. Ansbacher (Garden City, 1969), p. 1.
3. Quoted by Joseph Wortis in his *Fragments of an Analysis with Freud* (New York, 1954), p. 44.
4. Herbert Marcuse, "Obsolescence of the Freudian Concept of Man," in *Five Lectures* (Boston, 1970), p. 61.
5. Theodor W. Adorno, *Minima Moralia* (Frankfurt, 1964), p. 56.
6. James J. Putnam, "The Work of Alfred Adler Considered with Especial Reference to That of Freud" (1916), in Putnam, *Addresses on Psychoanalysis* (London, 1951), p. 314. Freud considered this article "an excellent rebuttal of Adler" (*A Psychoanalytic Dialogue: The Letters of Sigmund Freud and Karl Abraham* [London, 1965], p. 238). Cf. Fritz Wittels, "The Neo-Adlerians," *American Journal of Sociology*, 45 (1939), pp. 433 ff.: "Against Eros enthroned by Freud, he [Adler] invoked good old common sense" (p. 436).
7. Sigmund Freud, *New Introductory Lectures on Psychoanalysis* (New York, 1965), p. 142.
8. Freud, "From the History of an Infantile Neurosis," in *Three Case Studies*, ed. Philip Rieff (New York, 1963), p. 241 (emphasis added).
9. Freud, "On the History of the Psychoanalytic Movement," *Collected Papers* (London, 1957), vol. 1, p. 352.
10. Ernest Jones, *Life and Work of Sigmund Freud* (New York, 1955), vol. 2, p. 134. Considering only the immediate participants of the Adlerian-Freud break, Heinz L. Ansbacher — Adler's editor — denies there was any political meaning in it; see his remarks in Alfred Adler, *Superiority and Social Interest*, eds. Heinz L. and Rowena R. Ansbacher (New York, 1973), p. 345. Here at issue is more the wider political impact.
11. Henri F. Ellenberger, *Discovery of the Unconscious* (New York, 1970), p. 601. Cogent accounts of Adler are few and far between. The one in Ellenberger is by far the best; however, his attempt to explain Adler's lack of recognition is more than a bit strained. The biographical essay by Carl Furtmüller in Adler, *Superiority and Social Interest*, should also be mentioned. Hertha

Orgler, *Alfred Adler* (New York, 1965), and Phyllis Bottomore, *Alfred Adler* (London, 1957), are not particularly useful.

12. C. Furtmüller, in Adler, *Superiority and Social Interest,* p. 333.
13. Manès Sperber, *Alfred Adler oder das Elend der Psychologie* (Vienna, 1970), pp. 36–37. See Lou Andreas-Salomé's remarks about a conversation with Adler in *The Freud Journal of Lou Andreas-Salomé,* ed. Stanley A. Leavy (New York, 1964), p. 42.
14. Herman Nunberg and Ernst Federn, eds., *Minutes of the Vienna Psychoanalytic Society* (New York, 1967), vol. 2, pp. 172 ff.
15. *Heilen und Bilden,* hrsg. A. Adler (Munich, 1914), p. 104.
16. H. L. and R. R. Ansbacher, eds., *Individual Psychology of Alfred Adler* (New York, 1964), pp. 65 ff.
17. *Ibid.,* pp. 40–42.
18. Alice Rühle-Gerstel, *Freud und Adler* (Dresden, n.d. [1925?]), p. 96.
19. Adler, *The Neurotic Constitution* (London, 1918), pp. x, xii.
20. Adler, *Superiority and Social Interest,* pp. 216–17; 213.
21. Lewis Way, *Adler's Place in Psychology* (New York, 1950), p. 251.
22. Cited in Patrick Mullahy, *Oedipus: Myth and Complex* (New York, 1955), p. 124.
23. Adler, *Superiority and Social Interest,* p. 208.
24. Adorno, "Die revidierte Psychoanalyse," in Adorno, Horkheimer, and Marcuse, *Kritische Theorie der Gesellschaft* (n.p., n.d.), vol. 4, p. 31.
25. Taken from the minutes as cited by Kenneth M. Colby, "On the Disagreement Between Freud and Adler," *American Imago,* VIII, 3 (1951), pp. 233–35. See, for a good account of the split and these years in general, Vincent Brome, *Freud and His Early Circle* (New York, 1969).
26. Freud, "On the History of the Psychoanalytic Movement," *Collected Papers,* vol. 1, pp. 340–45.
27. Freud, *New Introductory Lectures on Psychoanalysis,* p. 142.
28. Adler, *Science of Living,* pp. 5, 8.
29. Adler, *Understanding Human Nature* (Greenwich, Connecticut, 1969), p. ix.
30. Freud, *General Introduction to Psychoanalysis* (New York, 1963), p. 441. Another example: "Sexual morality as society — and, at its most extreme — American society — defines it, seems very despicable to me. I stand for a much freer sexual life" (*James Jackson Putnam and Psychoanalysis: Letters Between*

Putnam and Sigmund Freud, ed. Nathan G. Hale [Cambridge, Massachusetts, 1971], p. 189).

31. Freud, *Future of an Illusion* (Garden City, 1964), pp. 15–16. For a different conceptualization of the radical content of Freud, see Philip Lichtenberg, *Psychoanalysis: Radical and Conservative* (New York, 1969).

32. See Sperber, *Alfred Adler,* pp. 278 ff.

33. Way, *Adler's Place in Psychology,* p. 265.

34. Adorno, "Die revidierte Psychoanalyse," p. 41.

35. Karl Marx, *Theories of Surplus Value* (Moscow, 1968), vol. 2, pp. 118–19.

36. *Ibid.* (Moscow, 1971), vol. 3, pp. 84–85.

37. Marx, *Grundrisse* (Middlesex, England, 1973), p. 884.

38. Cited in and see H. L. Ansbacher's introduction to Adler, *Superiority and Social Interest,* pp. 9–10.

39. Walter T. James, "Karen Horney and Erich Fromm in Relation to Alfred Adler," *Individual Psychology Bulletin,* VI (1947), pp. 105 ff. Cf. Nathan Freeman, "Concepts of Adler and Horney," *American Journal of Psychoanalysis,* X (1950), pp. 18 ff.

40. Clara Thompson, *Psychoanalysis: Evolution and Development* (New York, 1951), pp. 159, 199. Cf. Mullahy, *Oedipus: Myth and Complex,* pp. 324–25.

41. Horkheimer, "Ernst Simmel and Freudian Philosophy," *International Journal of Psychoanalysis,* 29 (1948), p. 111. Or Horkheimer wrote on Freud, "Psychology without libido is in no way psychology" (cited in Martin Jay, *The Dialectical Imagination: A History of the Frankfurt School* [Boston, 1973], p. 102).

42. N. Freeman, "Concepts of Adler and Horney," p. 25; and Floyd W. Matson, *The Broken Image* (Garden City, 1966), pp. 208 ff.

43. Marcuse, *Eros and Civilization* (New York, 1962), p. 52.

44. H. C. Abraham and E. L. Freud, eds., *Psycho-analytic Dialogue: The Letters of Sigmund Freud and Karl Abraham,* p. 12.

45. For a discussion of second nature, see Russell Jacoby, "Towards a Critique of Automatic Marxism: The Politics of Philosophy from Lukács to the Frankfurt School," *Telos,* 10 (1971), especially pp. 142 ff.

46. Marcuse, *Eros and Civilization,* p. 120.

47. Freud, "Thoughts for the Times on War and Death," *Collected Papers,* vol. 4, p. 297.

48. Cited in Jones, *Life and Work of Sigmund Freud,* vol. 2, p. 455.

49. Freud, "Why War?" *Collected Papers,* vol. 5, p. 275.

163 *Notes*

50. Freud, *Totem and Taboo* (New York, 1946), pp. 193, 185.
51. Freud, *The Ego and the Id* (New York, 1962), p. 26.
52. Ludwig Binswanger, *Sigmund Freud: Reminiscences of a Friendship* (New York, 1957), pp. 96–97. For the complete citation of Freud on Binswanger see the next chapter.
53. Marcuse, *Eros and Civilization*, p. 236.
54. Adorno, "Die revidierte Psychoanalyse," p. 30.
55. Institut für Sozialforschung, *Soziologische Exkurse* (Frankfurt, 1956), p. 42. This and subsequent sentences — "Er ist Mitmensch, ehe er auch Individuum ist . . ." — are missing in the English translation, Frankfurt Institute for Social Research, *Aspects of Sociology* (Boston, 1972), p. 40.
56. Horkheimer, in *Tensions That Cause War*, ed. Hadley Cantril (Urbana, Illinois, 1950), p. 38.
57. Marcuse, *Eros and Civilization*, p. 232. Marcuse's critique of the neo-Freudian revisionism first appeared in *Dissent* magazine in 1955, and then as an epilogue to *Eros and Civilization*. Here two other critiques of the neo-Freudians should be mentioned which in some respects converge with Marcuse's: Paul Goodman's "The Political Meaning of Some Recent Revisions of Freud," *Politics*, II (1945), pp. 197 ff.; and John Clarkson, "The Function of Anti-Sex: The Social Meaning of Dr. Erich Fromm's Ethical Desexualization of Psychoanalysis," *Contemporary Issue*, IX (1958), pp. 75 ff. The Clarkson essay could be characterized as a Reichian critique of Fromm. In this context the work of Robert Lindner from the 1950s, though somewhat dated, is worth mentioning; see his critique of Adler and the neo-Freudians in *The Revolutionist's Handbook* (New York, 1971), originally published in 1952 as *Prescription for Rebellion*.
58. Marcuse, *Eros and Civilization*, pp. 235–36.
59. Erich Fromm, "The Human Implications of Instinctivistic 'Radicalism,'" *Dissent*, II, 4 (1955), pp. 348, 349.
60. Marcuse, *Eros and Civilization*, pp. 228, 229.
61. Marcuse, "A Reply to Erich Fromm," *Dissent*, III, 1 (1956), p. 81.
62. Fromm, *The Art of Loving* (New York, 1963), pp. 109, 111.
63. Adorno, "Sociology and Psychology," *New Left Review*, 47 (1968), p. 95.
64. Marcuse, *Five Lectures*, p. 44.
65. Rudolf Hilferding, *Das Finanzkapital* (Frankfurt, 1973), Band II, p. 456.

66. Horkheimer, "Vernunft und Selbsterhaltung," in *Autoritärer Staat,* p. 102.

67. Adorno, "Sociology and Psychology," p. 95.

68. Adorno, *Kritik* (Frankfurt, 1971), p. 64.

69. Marcuse, *Five Lectures,* p. 60.

70. Frankfurt Institute, *Aspects of Sociology,* pp. 141–42.

71. Ellenberger, *Discovery of the Unconscious,* p. 645.

72. Robert White, "Adler and the Future of Ego Psychology," in *Essays in Individual Psychology,* eds. K. A. Adler and D. Deutsch (New York, 1959), p. 440.

73. Heinz Hartmann, *Ego Psychology and the Problem of Adaption* (New York, 1958), p. 6.

74. *Ibid.,* pp. 8, 81.

75. Adorno, "Sociology and Psychology," p. 91.

76. See Klaus Horn, "Insgeheim kulturistische Tendenzen der modernen psychoanalytischen Orthodoxie," in *Psychoanalyse als Sozialwissenschaft* (Frankfurt, 1971). More than most, Hartmann seemed aware of the problem; see H. Hartmann, "The Application of Psychoanalytic Concepts to Social Science," *Psychoanalytic Quarterly,* XIX, 3 (1950), pp. 385 ff.

77. Daniel Yankelovich and William Barrett, *Ego and Instinct* (New York, 1971), p. 97.

78. Paul Roazen, *Freud: Political and Social Thought* (New York, 1970), p. 234.

79. Henry M. Ruitenbeek, *Freud and America* (New York, 1966), p. 163.

80. Matson, *The Broken Image,* pp. 210–13. Matson's book illustrates the insufficiency of neo-Adlerian theory which finally turns ideological. While the book is openly and cogently critical of behaviorism, it enthusiastically returns to the establishment fold when it comes to the Freud/Adler–neo-Freudian divergence. Matson denigrates the interpretation of Freud by Marcuse, Brown, et al., by calling the latter "literary figures" — the first and final insult of the positivist protecting his scientific turf from the unaccredited outsiders; he tells us that their thought "betrays the vast difference separating this essentially literary perspective from the clinical professional center of psychoanalysis" (pp. 190–91). Matson thinks that he is scoring a decisive point against Freudians such as Marcuse when he notes several times that they are in the minority as compared with the compact majority of the neo-Freudians and Adlerians: in a book

claiming to be critical and humanist he is confident that in thought majority rules. "The romantic revival [Marcuse et al.] *is moving in a direction diametrically opposite to the main current of psychoanalytic thought*" (p. 191, Matson's emphasis). In his attachment to the "mainstream" and majority thought Matson unwittingly tells the truth about the Freud-Adler exchange as it has persisted till the present. "From the perspective of our own day, it might even be argued . . . that it was the turn first taken by Adler some fifty years ago which has come to be the 'mainstream' of the psychoanalytic movement — and that taken by Freud which has been in fact the 'deviation'" (p. 194). Exactly.

81. Freud, *The Problem of Anxiety* (New York, 1963), pp. 22–23, 25.
82. Freud, *The Ego and the Id*, p. 1.
83. Cited in Max Schur, *The Id and the Regulatory Principles of Mental Functioning* (London, 1957), pp. 17–18.
84. See Otto Fenichel's model discussion of ego and depth moments, such as in his "Ego Disturbances and Their Treatment," *Collected Papers of Otto Fenichel: Second Series* (New York, 1954).
85. Marcuse, *Eros and Civilization*, p. 30.
86. Adorno, "Sociology and Psychology," p. 88.
87. Adorno, *Kritik*, p. 37 .
88. Freud, *Group Psychology and the Analysis of the Ego* (New York, 1960), p. 3.
89. Adorno, *Kritik*, pp. 90–91.
90. Adorno, "Sociology and Psychology," p. 88.

III   Conformist Psychology

1. Erich Fromm, *The Sane Society* (Greenwich, Connecticut, 1955), p. 174 (Fromm's emphasis).
2. Sigmund Freud, "Future Prospects of Psychoanalytic Therapy," *Collected Papers* (London, 1957), vol. 2, p. 290.
3. Cited in Roman Rosdolsky, *Zur Entstehungsgeschichte des Marxschen 'Kapital'* (Frankfurt and Vienna, 1968), Band I, p. 358.
4. Carl Rogers, *On Encounter Groups* (New York, 1970), p. 162.
5. Gordon W. Allport, *Becoming* (New Haven, 1955), pp. 68, 72.
6. See Michel Foucault, *Madness and Civilization* (New York, 1963), especially pp. 42–77.
7. Fromm, *The Art of Loving* (New York, 1963), pp. 4, 90 ff.

8. Rollo May, *Man's Search for Himself* (New York, 1967), p. viii.
9. *Ibid.*, pp. 135–36, 232–33.
10. May, Allport, et al., *Existential Psychology* (New York, 1961), p. 60 and passim.
11. Walter Kaufmann, ed., *Hegel: Texts and Commentary* (Garden City, 1966), p. 18.
12. G. W. F. Hegel, *Werk 2: Janaer Schriften* (Frankfurt, 1970), p. 548.
13. Fromm, *Man for Himself* (Greenwich, Connecticut, 1947), p. v.
14. Allport, *Personality and Social Encounter* (Boston, 1964), p. 140.
15. Theodor W. Adorno, *Prisms*, transl. Samuel and Shierry Weber (London, 1967), p. 25.
16. Viktor E. Frankl, *Psychotherapy and Existentialism* (New York, 1967), p. 18.
17. Ludwig Binswanger, *Sigmund Freud: Reminiscences of a Friendship* (New York, 1957), pp. 96–97.
18. Allport, *Personality and Social Encounter*, p. 105.
19. Freud, "Five Lectures on Psychoanalysis," *Standard Edition* (London, 1957), vol. 11, p. 50.
20. Abraham H. Maslow, *Toward a Psychology of Being* (Princeton, 1968), pp. 25, 156. As one of Maslow's devotees writes: "[Maslow's paper on self-actualization] is revolutionary because this is the first time a psychologist has ignored the assumption that underlies all Freudian psychology: that psychology, like medicine, is basically a study of the sick" (Colin Wilson, *New Pathways in Psychology: Maslow and the Post-Freudian Revolution* [New York, 1972], p. 171). Compare this with Carl Rogers's formulation: "One of the most revolutionary concepts to grow out of our clinical experience is the growing recognition that the innermost core of man's nature, the deepest layers of his personality, the base of his 'animal nature,' is positive in nature — is basically socialized, forward-moving, rational and realistic" (Carl Rogers, *On Becoming a Person* [Boston, 1961], p. 91).
21. Frank Goble, *The Third Force: The Psychology of Abraham Maslow* (New York, 1971), p. 55.
22. Allport, *Becoming*, pp. 49 ff.; 75–76.
23. Frankl, *Psychotherapy and Existentialism*, p. 18.
24. Maslow, *Toward a Psychology of Being*, p. 124.
25. Cited in Theodor Reik, *From Thirty Years with Freud* (New York, 1940), p. 138.

26. For a good presentation of German positivism and conservatism see Karl Mannheim, "Conservative Thought," in *Essays on Sociology and Social Psychology* (New York, 1953).

27. Cited in Marcuse, *Reason and Revolution* (Boston, 1960), p. 346.

28. Karl Marx, "The Philosophical Manifesto of the Historical School of Law," in *Writings of the Young Marx on Philosophy and Society,* eds. Lloyd D. Easton and Kurt H. Guddat (Garden City, 1967), p. 98.

29. See, for example, Emile Durkheim, *Socialism* (New York, 1962), especially pp. 239 ff. and the introduction by Alvin Gouldner, pp. 26 ff.

30. Marcuse, "Existentialism: Remarks on Jean-Paul Sartre's *L'Être et le néant,*" *Journal of Philosophy and Phenomenological Research,* II, 4 (June 1942), pp. 323, 324.

31. Adorno, *Jargon der Eigentlichkeit* (Frankfurt, 1964), p. 52.

32. Adorno, "Sociology and Psychology," *New Left Review,* 47 (1968), p. 81.

33. Adorno, *Stichworte* (Frankfurt, 1969), p. 44.

34. See the discussion of second nature in the previous chapter.

35. Adorno, *Minima Moralia* (Frankfurt, 1964), pp. 75–76.

36. Cf. Adorno, *Negativ Dialektik* (Frankfurt, 1970), pp. 330 ff.

37. Rogers, *On Encounter Groups,* p. 135.

38. Adorno, "Society," *Salmagundi,* 10–11 (Fall 1969–Winter 1970), p. 148.

39. Rarely is the mixture of the progressive and regressive moments of a critique of classification as clear as in some of the work of Thomas Szasz; on the one hand there is a progressive critique of classifications of the mentally "ill" which, however, because it is based on an individualistic nominalist philosophy tilts over into ideology: praise of bourgeois individualism. "To classify human behavior is to constrain it" (*Ideology and Insanity* [Garden City, 1970], p. 201). This leads Szasz to attack as "collectivistic" community health programs.

40. Adorno, *Aufsätze zur Gesellschaftstheorie und Methodologie* (Frankfurt, 1970), p. 93.

41. Frankfurt Institute for Social Research, *Aspects of Sociology* (Boston, 1972), p. 123; and Institut für Sozialforschung, *Soziologische Exkurse* (Frankfurt, 1956), p. 111.

42. Adorno et al., *The Authoritarian Personality* (New York, 1969), p. 747.

43. See the discussion in J. Matzner, "Der Begriff der Charaktermaske bei Karl Marx," *Sozial Welt*, XV (1964), pp. 130 ff.
44. B. F. Skinner, "Beyond Freedom and Dignity," in *Psychology Today*, V, 3 (August 1971), p. 39.
45. A graphic example of the antinomies of behaviorism is Harold L. Cohn, James Filipczak, *A New Learning Environment*, forewords by R. Buckminster Fuller and B. F. Skinner (San Francisco and Washington, 1971). Again, there is the same confident materialism. "The youngster is not mentally bankrupt, but the public school and the systems that sustain it are" (p. 5). And again there is the same undisguised enthusiasm for the capitalist ethos of success and calculation which is billed as a recent scientific innovation. "Using money as a generalized reinforcer worked in our educational research environment, just as it does in our society. We all perform because there is something in it for us" (p. 8). The goal is to move the delinquent youth toward the "middle-class adolescent life" (p. 141).
46. Spiro T. Agnew, "Blast at Behaviorism," *Psychology Today*, V, 8 (January 1972), pp. 4 ff.
47. Wilson, *New Pathways in Psychology*, p. 181. Wilson also notes that while Marcuse was apparently uninterested in Maslow's ideas, they *were* having influence where it mattered — in corporation board rooms" (p. 183).
48. Maslow, *Eupsychian Management* (Homewood, Illinois, 1965), p. 206.

IV   Negative Psychoanalysis and Marxism

1. Heinrich Regius (Max Horkheimer), *Dämmerung* (Zürich, 1934), p. 135.
2. Horkheimer, "Vernunft und Selbsterhaltung," in *Autoritärer Staat* (Amsterdam, 1968), p. 91.
3. An unfortunately excellent example of this is Shulamith Firestone's *The Dialectic of Sex* (New York, 1970). Her synthesis of Freud and Marx as crystallized in the concept "sex class" is geometrically perfect and theoretically vacuous. Her book suffers from a host of lethal simplifications about both Marxism and psychoanalysis; see the critical review in *Telos*, 8 (1971), pp. 149 ff.

4. Helmut Dahmer, "Psychoanalyse und historischer Materialismus," in *Psychoanalyse als Sozialwissenschaft* (Frankfurt, 1971), p. 64.

5. Horkheimer, *Autoritärer Staat,* p. 59. An English translation is now in *Telos,* 15 (1973), pp. 11 ff.

6. Cited in "Introduction" by Fred Halliday in Karl Korsch, *Marxism and Philosophy* (London, 1970), pp. 9–10.

7. Wilhelm Reich, *People in Trouble* (Rangeley, Maine, 1953), p. 59.

8. For a brief survey of the Russian reception to psychoanalysis, see Joseph Wortis, *Soviet Psychiatry* (Middlesex, England, 1950), pp. 72 ff.

9. W. Jurinetz, "Psychoanalyse und Marxismus," in *Psychoanalyse und Marxismus,* hrsg. H. J. Sandkühler (Frankfurt, 1970), pp. 85–86.

10. Karl Korsch, *Schriften zur Sozialisierung* (Frankfurt, 1969), pp. 74–75.

11. Georg Lukács, *Geschichte und Klassenbewusstsein* (Amsterdam, 1967), pp. 86–88, and *History and Class Consciousness* (London, 1971), pp. 73–75. See Lukács's comments on mass psychology in his review of Michels's *Zur Soziologie des Parteiwesens,* reprinted in Lukács, *Organisation und Partei* (n.p., n.d.). He says there mass psychology is "nothing but the scientific wish-dream of the bourgeoisie." Illustrative of the fissure between the psychological and historical dimensions in Lukács are his astounding personal remarks in an interview shortly before his death; these, perhaps, illuminate his defective analysis of much of modern literature, to say nothing of his anti-psychological political thought. "I must say that I am perhaps not a very contemporary man. I can say that I have never felt frustration or any kind of complex in my life. I know what these mean, of course, from the literature of the twentieth century, and from having read Freud. But I have not experienced them myself" (Georg Lukács, "An Unofficial Interview," *New Left Review,* 68 [1971], p. 58). Compare these remarks with those recorded by Gyula Illyés: "What preserves me is that I have no inner life. I am interested in everything except my soul" (Gyula Illyés, "On Charon's Ferry," *New Hungarian Quarterly,* XIII [1972], p. 154).

12. See Klaus Horn, "Psychoanalyse — Anpassungslehre oder kri-

tische Theorie des Subjekts?" in *Marxismus. Psychoanalyse. Sexpol 2,* hrsg. H.-P. Gente (Frankfurt, 1972), pp. 116 ff.

13. Theodor W. Adorno, "Postscriptum," in Adorno, *Aufsätze zur Gesellschaftstheorie* (Frankfurt, 1970), p. 55.

14. Adorno, *Stichworte* (Frankfurt, 1969), pp. 182–83.

15. It should be recalled that Ernst Bloch's 1923 review of *History and Class Consciousness* took it to task exactly for its sociologism, though this was not argued from within a psychoanalytic context. Lukács, according to Bloch, in his drive toward totality, loses the "depth-relations of being"; this was due to a "reduction or homogenization to a pure *social* matter" or to a "certain simplistic tendency to . . . an almost exclusive sociological homogenization of the [historical] process" (Ernst Bloch, "Aktualität und Utopie. Zu Lukács' 'Geschichte und Klassenbewusstein'" reprinted in *Lukacsdebatte* [Marxismus-Kollektiv, 1969], pp. 136–38). See the discussion and relevant citations in Paul Breines, "Bloch Magic," *Continuum,* VII, 4 (1970), pp. 622–24.

16. Adorno, *Negativ Dialektik* (Frankfurt, 1970), p. 343.

17. Adorno, *Stichworte,* p. 159.

18. Karl Marx, "Communist Manifesto," in Marx and Engels's *Basic Writings on Politics and Philosophy,* ed. Lewis S. Feuer (Garden City, 1959), p. 22. "It is not individuals who are set free by free competition; it is, rather, capital which is set free" (Marx, *Grundrisse* [Middlesex, England, 1973], p. 650).

19. Adorno, *Negativ Dialektik,* p. 171.

20. Marx, "Contributions to the Critique of Hegel's Philosophy of Right," in *Marx and Engels on Religion* (New York, 1964), p. 42.

21. For a lengthier discussion of the political and philosophical meaning of automatic Marxism, see my "Towards a Critique of Automatic Marxism: The Politics of Philosophy from Lukács to the Frankfurt School," *Telos,* 10 (1971). Cf. Paul Breines, "Praxis and Its Theorists," *Telos,* 11 (1972), pp. 82 ff.

22. Herbert Marcuse, *Five Lectures* (Boston, 1970), pp. 38–39.

23. Marcuse, *Eros and Civilization* (New York, 1962), p. 83.

24. Sigmund Freud, *New Introductory Lectures on Psychoanalysis* (New York, 1965), p. 181.

25. Ernst L. Freud, ed., *Letters of Sigmund Freud and Arnold Zweig* (London, 1970), p. 21. If Freud was pessimistic about the possibility for change, this should be measured against Theodor Reik's pessimism. Reik accused Freud's *Future of an Illusion*

of suffering from the optimistic hope for a changed future. Freud responded by saying that he did not consider Reik's "pessimistic dismissal of a better future" justified (Theodor Reik, *Freud als Kulturkritiker* [Vienna, 1930], pp. 26, 64).

26. S. Freud, *Civilization and Its Discontents* (New York, 1962), pp. 59 ff.
27. S. Freud, *New Introductory Lectures,* p. 67.
28. Emphasis added. Cited by Ernest Jones, *Life and Work of Sigmund Freud* (New York, 1957), vol. 3, p. 345. For a recent discussion that collects most of the relevant Freud passages, see W. Lepenies and H. Nolte, *Kritik der Anthropologie. Marx und Freud* (Munich, 1971).
29. According to his son, Federn was a member of the Austrian Social Democracy till its dissolution in 1934 (see Ernst Federn, "Funfunddressig Jahr mit Freud," *Psyche,* XXV (1971), p. 723.
30. Paul Federn, "Zur Psychologie der Revolution," reprinted in *Psychoanalyse Marxismus und Sozialwissenschaft* (W. Grauenhage, 1971), pp. 412, 418.
31. *Ibid.,* p. 416.
32. *Ibid.,* pp. 417, 429.
33. Erich Fromm, "Psychoanalytic Characterology . . . ," reprinted in *Crisis in Psychoanalysis* (Greenwich, Connecticut, 1971), p. 177.
34. Horkheimer et al., *Studien über Autorität und Familie* (Paris, 1936), p. 87.
35. Wilhelm Reich, *Character Analysis,* 3d ed. (New York, 1949), pp. xxii, xxv (emphasis deleted from original).
36. Reich, *Geschlechtsreife, Enthaltsamkeit, Ehemoral* (Berlin, 1968), p. 61.
37. Horkheimer, "Geschichte u. Psychologie," reprinted in *Kritische Theorie der Gesellschaft* (Frankfurt, 1968), I, pp. 19–20.
38. Horkheimer, "Autorität und Familie," in *Kritische Theorie der Gesellschaft,* I, pp. 288, 330.
39. Adorno, *Stichworte,* p. 132.
40. Adorno et al., *The Authoritarian Personality* (New York, 1969), p. 749.
41. Adorno, "Die revidierte Psychoanalyse," in Adorno, Horkheimer, and Marcuse, *Kritische Theorie der Gesellschaft* (n.p., n.d.), IV, pp. 27–28.
42. Marcuse, *Five Lectures,* pp. 13–14. One of the most interesting attempts to work out the relationship between a Marxist notion of reification and a psychological or clinical one, perhaps to be

found in some forms of schizophrenia, is Joseph Gabel's *La fausse conscience* (Paris, 1962). A discussion of this book cannot take place here; only to be noted is that any such discussion would have to pursue the difference between Lukács's and Mannheim's notions of ideology, as Gabel sees his work as validating the "total" or "universal" notion, that is, Mannheim's. Some of his formulations that derive from this seem questionable.

43. Aurel Kolnai, *Psychoanalysis and Society* (London, 1921), pp. 116, 173.

44. Herman Nunberg and Ernst Federn, eds., *Minutes of the Vienna Psychoanalytic Society* (New York, 1962), vol. 1, p. 162.

45. *Ibid.*, p. 164.

46. The following is concerned with the German debate; there were others of less interest, such as the insular English examination of Marx and Freud. See Reuben Osborn, *Freud and Marx: A Dialectical Study* (London, 1937), arguing for the use of psychoanalysis within Marxism; and a rejoinder, Francis Bartlett, *Sigmund Freud: A Marxian Study* (London, 1938). A presentation of this exchange, which is as insular as the original, is to be found in Thomas Johnston, *Freud and Political Thought* (New York, 1965), pp. 81 ff. Later English contributions are of interest because they explicitly take up the question of whether the neo-Freudian revisions render psychoanalysis more or less acceptable to Marxism; some of the main essays in this are F. Bartlett, "Recent Trends in Psychoanalysis," *Science and Society*, IX, 3 (Summer 1945), pp. 214 ff.; Marie Carroll, "On Bartlett's Psychoanalytic Views," *Science and Society*, IX, 4 (Fall 1945), pp. 362 ff.; Joseph Wortis, "Freud, Horney, Fromm and Others," *Science and Society*, X, 2 (Spring 1946), pp. 176 ff.; Judson T. Stone, "The Theory and Practice of Psychoanalysis," *Science and Society*, X, 1 (Winter 1946), pp. 54 ff. Finally to be mentioned here is the intelligent essay by Paul Baran, *Marxism and Psychoanalysis* (New York, 1960).

47. Works on Reich are appearing thick and fast. A decent exposition is to be found in Constantin Sinelnikoff, *L'oeuvre de Wilhelm Reich*, 2 vols. (Paris, 1970). Others, in order of descending quality, are Jean-Michel Palmier, *Wilhelm Reich* (Paris, 1969); Michel Cattier, *La vie et l'oeuvre du Docteur Wilhelm Reich* (Lausanne, n.d.); Paul Robinson, *The Freudian Left* (New York, 1969). The last is superficial, uninformed, and defective.

One example: in a book solely concerned with Reich, Róheim, and Marcuse, Robinson does not seem to be aware that Reich wrote extensively on Róheim. A better treatment, though with a different focus, is Richard King's *The Party of Eros* (New York, 1973). For some other details on Reich, see Ilse O. Reich, *Wilhelm Reich* (New York, 1970), and Ola Raknes, *Wilhelm Reich and Orgonomy* (Middlesex, England, 1971).

48. W. Reich, "Dialectical Materialism and Psychoanalysis," in *Studies on the Left*, VI, 4 (1966), pp. 6–7.

49. *Ibid.*, pp. 11, 36–37.

50. E. Fromm, "Politik und Psychoanalyse," *Psychoanalytische Bewegung*, III, 5 (1931), p. 444.

51. Fromm, "Method and Function of an Analytic Social Psychology," reprinted in *Crisis of Psychoanalysis* (Greenwich, Connecticut, 1971), p. 155 (emphasis deleted).

52. Otto Fenichel, "Über die Psychoanalyse als Keim einer zukünftigen dialektische-materialistischen Psychologie," *Zeitschrift für politische Psychologie und Sexualökonomie*, I, 1 (1934), pp. 49–50 (emphasis deleted).

53. As has been often noted, the changes in editions of Reich's book are a major obstacle in pursuing his thought; even aside from often crucial revisions in translation, there are frequent major alterations to earlier editions. The new edition (1970) of *The Mass Psychology of Fascism* not only eliminates the important preface to the first edition and the afterword to the second, but adds some 200 pages. Recently some translations based on the original editions appeared: see Wilhelm Reich, *Sex-Pol Essays 1929–1934*, ed. Lee Baxandall (New York, 1972).

54. Reich, "The Imposition of Sexual Morality," in *Sex-Pol*, p. 245.

55. Reich, *Massenpsychologie des Faschismus*, II. Auflage (n.p., n.d.), p. 5.

56. Reich, *People in Trouble*, p. 153.

57. See "Zur Geschichte des Sex-Pol-Bewegung," *Zeitschrift für politische Psychologie* . . . I, 3–4 (1934), pp. 260 ff.

58. Reich, "Nachwort zur II Auflage," *Massenpsychologie des Faschismus*, pp. 277 ff.

59. Cf. C. Sinelnikov, "Early 'Marxist' Critiques of Reich," *Telos*, 13 (1972), pp. 131 ff.

60. I. Sapir, "Freudismus, Soziologie, Psychologie," in *Psychoanalyse und Marxismus*, hrsg. Hans Jörg Sandkühler, p. 223.

61. Reich, "Zur Anwendung der Psychoanalyse in der Geschichts-forschung," *Zeitschrift für politische Psychologie* . . . I, 1 (1934), pp. 8, 15.
62. Siegfried Bernfeld, "Die kommunistische Diskussion um die Psychoanalyse und Reich's 'Widerlegung' der Todestriebhypothese," in *Psychoanalyse und Marxismus*, p. 279. Reich considered the introduction of the death instinct and repetition compulsion as "undoubtedly metaphysic element, a hypothesis which was not only unproven but incapable of proof" (Reich, *Character Analysis*, 3d ed. [New York, 1949], p. 215).
63. Bernfeld, "Die kommunistische Diskussion . . . ," p. 283.
64. Reich, *Character Analysis*, pp. 159 ff.
65. Reich, "Überblich über das Forschungsgebiet der Sexualökonomie," *Zeitschrift für politische Psychologie* . . . II (1935), pp. 5, 6. Cf. Howard Press, "The Marxism and Anti-Marxism of Reich," *Telos*, 9 (1971), pp. 65 ff. For a critique of Reich's positivism and fetish of genital sexuality, see H. Dahmer, "Wilhelm Reich. Seine Stellung zu Freud und Marx," in *Marxismus. Psychoanalyse. Sexpol 2*, hrsg. H.-P. Gente, pp. 80 ff. Also see H. Dahmer, "Psychoanalyse und historischer Materialismus," in *Psychoanalyse als Sozialwissenschaft;* this last essay is a cogent and intelligent articulation of the Frankfurt School position. For a sympathetic discussion of Reich, see Bertell Ollmann, "The Marxism of Wilhelm Reich," in *The Unknown Dimension: European Marxism Since Lenin*, eds. Dick Howard and Karl L. Klare (New York, 1972), pp. 197 ff. The full flavor of where a reactionary Reichian position can lead can be sampled in Elsworth Baker, *Man in the Trap* (New York, 1967), a book dedicated to Reich. "Only the most 'hideous distortions' of orgonomic truth — as Reich put it — could possibly equate his work, thinking, and hopes for mankind with those of present-day liberals, leftists, and beatnik-bohemians" (p. xiii).
66. Eric Pfeiffer, ed., *Sigmund Freud and Lou Andreas-Salomé: Letters* (New York, 1972), p. 174.
67. Fromm in a review of Reich, *Der Einbruch der Sexualmoral* in *Zeitschrift für Sozialforschung*, II (1933), pp. 119 ff.
68. Horkheimer, "Egoismus und Freiheitsbewegung" (1936), reprinted in *Traditionelle und Kritische Theorie. Vier Aufsätze* (Frankfurt, 1970), p. 154.
69. Marcuse, *Eros and Civilization*, p. 218, and *Counterrevolution and Revolt* (Boston, 1972), p. 130.

70. Sandor Ferenczi, "The Ontogenesis of the Interest in Money," in Ferenczi, *Sex in Psychoanalysis* and *The Development of Psychoanalysis* (with Otto Rank), (New York, 1956), p. 276.

71. Fenichel, "The Drive to Amass Wealth," *Psychoanalytic Quarterly*, VII (1938), pp. 83, 85, 95. Cf. Fenichel's critique of Laforque's psychological reductionism (Fenichel, "Psychoanalyse der Politik. Eine Kritik," *Psychoanalytische Bewegung*, IV, 3 [1932], pp. 255 ff.). Laforque seeks "to understand the fate and present difficulties of capitalism without entering into the relations of production and their problematic" (p. 266).

72. Others, such as Franz Alexander, criticized both psychologism and sociologism within psychoanalysis. It may have been Alexander who initiated the use of the term "revisionists" to refer to the neo-Freudians (see Franz Alexander, "Psychoanalysis Revised," *Psychoanalytic Quarterly*, IX [1940], pp. 1 ff).

73. Fenichel, "Psychoanalytic Remarks on Fromm's 'Escape from Freedom,'" *The Psychoanalytic Review*, XXXI (1944), p. 150.

74. *Ibid.*, pp. 140 ff.

75. Fenichel's review of Horney, *New Ways in Psychoanalysis*, in *Psychoanalytic Quarterly*, IX (1940), p. 121.

76. Adorno, "Sociology and Psychology," *New Left Review*, 47 (1968), pp. 86, 93.

77. Adorno, *Zur Metakritik der Erkenntnistheorie* (Stuttgart, 1956), pp. 87–88.

78. Adorno, *Vorlesung zur Einleiting in die Erkenntnistheorie* (Frankfurt, n.d.), p. 102.

79. Adorno, *Aufsätze zur Gesellschaftstheorie*, p. 191.

80. Horkheimer, "Ernst Simmel and Freudian Philosophy," *International Journal of Psychoanalysis*, 29 (1948), p. 112.

81. Nathan G. Hale, ed., *James Jackson Putnam and Psychoanalysis: Letters Between Putnam and Sigmund Freud*... (Cambridge, Massachusetts, 1971), p. 171.

82. Quoted by Wortis, *Fragments of an Analysis with Freud*, p. 22.

83. Horkheimer, "Vernunft und Selbsterhaltung," pp. 100–01.

84. This is true with the important exception of Marcuse, who has attempted to work out a positive relation between a psychic and historical dimension.

85. Cf. F. Böckelmann, *Die schlechte Aufhebung der autoritären Persönlichkeit* (Frankfurt, 1971).

86. Marcuse, *One-Dimensional Man* (Boston, 1964), pp. 56 ff.

87. Adorno, "Sexualtabus und Recht heute," *Eingriffe* (Frankfurt, 1963), p. 101.

V The Politics of Subjectivity

1. René Descartes, "Discourse on Method," part III, in *Philosophical Writings*, Norman K. Smith (New York, 1958), p. 113.
2. Karl Marx, *Grundrisse* (Middlesex, England, 1973), p. 158.
3. Marx, *The Economic and Philosophic Manuscripts of 1844*, ed. Dirk J. Struik (New York, 1964), pp. 137–38.
4. Theodor W. Adorno, "Marginalien zu Theorie und Praxis," *Stichworte* (Frankfurt, 1969), p. 177.
5. Max Horkheimer, "Authorität und Familie," *Kritische Theorie der Gesellschaft*, Band I (Frankfurt, 1969), p. 346.
6. Adorno, *Negativ Dialektik* (Frankfurt, 1970), p. 148.
7. See Marx's comments on Bakunin's program in Marx and Engels, *Werke* (Berlin, 1969), vol. 18, pp. 14 ff.
8. Herbert Marcuse, "Neue Quellen zur Grundlegung des Historischen Materialismus," *Ideen zu Einer Kritischen Theorie* (Frankfurt, 1967), pp. 35 ff. English translation in Marcuse, *Studies in Critical Philosophy* (Boston, 1973).
9. Marx, *Civil War in France* (New York, 1940), p. 61.
10. Cf. Marx, *Capital* (Moscow, 1961), vol. 1, p. 763.
11. Marx, *The Economic and Philosophic Manuscripts of 1844*, pp. 132–33.
12. Marx and Engels, *The Holy Family* (Moscow, 1956), pp. 156–57.
13. Marquis de Sade, *Justine, Philosophy of the Bedroom* (New York, 1966), pp. 318–19, 321.
14. Marx, *Critique of the Gotha Programme* (New York, 1966), p. 10.
15. For a good discussion of Marxism and monogamy, see the work from the 1920s by the Russian scholar David Riazanov, available in French translation: "Communisme et marriage," *Partisans*, 32–33 (1966), pp. 69 ff.
16. See the letter of Marx to Jenny Marx cited in Alfred Schmidt, *Der Begriff der Natur in der Lehre von Marx* (Frankfurt, 1967), p. 113.
17. Yet if utopian thought is in order there is nowhere better to turn than to the most determined foe of bourgeois sexuality and civilization, Charles Fourier, and especially to his long-suppressed work, *Le nouveau monde amoureux* (Paris, 1967). Of particular interest is his notion of "pivotal love" (pp. 290 ff.) — a love

relation which is neither "simple fidelity" nor indifferent and brutal interchangeability. And see Freud's comments to Wortis: "We don't know what the future of monogamy will be, and cannot prophesy. . . . If socialism comes, we shall see what happens" (Joseph Wortis, *Fragments of an Analysis with Freud* [New York, 1954], p. 42).

18. Sigmund Freud, *Group Psychology and the Analysis of the Ego* (New York, 1960), p. 93.

19. Freud, *Civilization and Its Discontents* (New York, 1971), p. 55.

20. Horkheimer, "Vernunft und Selbsterhaltung," in *Autoritärer Staat* (Amsterdam, 1968), pp. 111, 113. Cf. the beautiful aphorism of Adorno, "Constanz," *Minima Moralia* (Frankfurt, 1964), p. 226. It is translated in Reimut Reiche, *Sexuality and Class Struggle* (London, 1970), p. 163.

21. Adorno, *Negativ Dialektik*, p. 278.

22. Georg Lukács, *Geschichte und Klassenbewusstein* (Amsterdam, 1967), p. 267; *History and Class Consciousness* (London, 1971), p. 262.

VI Theory and Therapy I: Freud

1. Sigmund Freud, cited by Helmut Dahmer in a review of B. Goetz, *Erinnerungen an Sigmund Freud,* in *Psyche,* XXIV (1970), p. 132.

2. Herbert Marcuse, *Eros and Civilization* (New York, 1962), p. 7.

3. *Ibid.,* p. 226. Cf. Stanley E. Hyman, "Psychoanalysis and the Climate of Tragedy," in *Freud and the Twentieth Century,* ed. Benjamin Nelson (New York, 1957).

4. Dieter Wyss, *Depth Psychology: A Critical History* (New York, 1966), pp. 317–18. This book is worth consulting, as it is encyclopedic in its scope.

5. For Fromm's latest misunderstanding of this point — and attack on Marcuse — see *The Crisis of Psychoanalysis* (Greenwich, Connecticut, 1971), pp. 25 ff.

6. Norman O. Brown, *Life Against Death* (New York, 1959), p. 155.

7. Theodor W. Adorno, "Sociology and Psychology," *New Left Review,* 46 (1967), p. 78.

8. Josef Breuer and Sigmund Freud, *Studies in Hysteria* (Boston, 1964), p. 232.

9. Freud, "Analysis Terminable and Interminable," *Collected Papers* (London, 1957), vol. 5, p. 329.

10. "Freudian theory cannot in any way be reduced to that neopositivist schema. The theory is not the simple systematization of observations. It remains the theory of interpretations" (Octave Mannoni, *Freud* [New York, 1971], pp. 143–44). "Psychoanalytic theory cannot . . . be reduced to a mere array of individual observations, nor does psychoanalytic theory represent a structure of thought superimposed upon the 'empirical material' that would have precedence" (Heinz Hartmann, Ernst Kris, and Rudolph M. Loewenstein, "The Function of Theory in Psychoanalysis," in *Drives, Affects, Behavior*, ed. R. M. Loewenstein [New York, 1953], p. 14).

11. Freud, *New Introductory Lectures on Psychoanalysis* (New York, 1965), pp. 156–57. "I did not like the idea that psychoanalysis should suddenly become fashionable because of purely practical considerations" (Freud to Abraham, in *A Psycho-analytic Dialogue: The Letters of Sigmund Freud and Karl Abraham*, ed. H. C. Abraham and E. L. Freud [London, 1965], pp. 279–80).

12. S. Freud, *The Question of Lay Analysis* (Garden City, 1964), p. 96.

13. Freud and Oskar Pfister, *Psychoanalysis and Faith: Letters of Freud and Pfister* (New York, 1963), p. 126. Here, too, it could be noted, Reich's positivist bent set him in opposition to Freud; he considered lay analysis a deviation from the natural scientific rigor of analysis (Cf. *Reich Speaks of Freud*, eds. Mary Higgins and Chester Raphael [New York, 1967], pp. 86–87).

14. Freud, *The Question of Lay Analysis*, p. 106.

15. Smiley Blanton, *Diary of My Analysis with Sigmund Freud* (New York, 1971), p. 116.

16. For a discussion of American reception and dilution of psychoanalysis see Nathan G. Hale, *Freud and the Americans: The Beginnings of Psychoanalysis in the United States* (New York, 1971), pp. 322 ff.; and John Burnham, *Psychoanalysis and American Medicine*, Monograph No. 20, *Psychological Issues*, V (1967), pp. 180 ff. Cf. Clarence P. Oberndorf, *A History of Psychoanalysis in America* (New York, 1964), p. 231. For a study that is not concerned with psychoanalysis, but illuminates the American interpretation of psychoanalysis, see Donald Meyer, *The Positive Thinkers* (Garden City, 1965).

17. Franz Alexander, *The Western Mind in Transition* (New York, 1960), p. 99. Freud repeated this in his "autobiography"; in America psychoanalysis "has suffered a great deal from being watered down" (*An Autobiographical Study* [New York, 1963], p. 100). For some other remarks of Freud on America, see Paul Roazen, *Freud: Political and Social Thought* (New York, 1970), pp. 97 ff.

18. Cited in Ernest Jones, *Life and Work of Sigmund Freud* (New York, 1957), vol. 3, p. 77.

19. Cited in Franz Alexander, ed., *Psychoanalytic Pioneers* (New York, 1966), p. 228.

20. H. D., *Tribute to Freud* (New York, 1956), p. 25.

21. Freud, *The Origins of Psychoanalysis: Letters of Wilhelm Fleiss* (New York, 1954), p. 162.

22. Abram Kardiner, "Freud — The Man I Knew," in Benjamin Nelson, ed., *Freud and the Twentieth Century* (New York, 1957), p. 52.

23. Cited in Alexander, *Psychoanalytic Pioneers*, p. 255.

24. See the discussion in *Psychoanalysis and Faith: Letters of Freud and Pfister*, pp. 119–20.

25. Freud, "Sandor Ferenczi (1933)," *Standard Edition* (London, 1964), vol. 12, p. 229. See Freud's remarks on Ferenczi's — and Rank's — innovations in *A Psycho-analytic Dialogue: The Letters of Sigmund Freud and Karl Abraham*, pp. 344 ff. These remarks also put into question charges about Freud's alleged despotism in theoretical matters.

26. Freud, *New Introductory Lectures*, p. 153.

27. Freud cited in P. Roazen, *Brother Animal: The Story of Freud and Tausk* (New York, 1969), p. 184. No one should look at Roazen's book without consulting its full-scale critique and rebuttal, Kurt R. Eissler, *Talent and Genius: The Fictitious Case of Tausk Contra Freud* (New York, 1971).

28. Freud, *General Introduction to Psychoanalysis* (New York, 1963), pp. 390–91.

29. Freud, "Future Prospects of Psychoanalytic Therapy," *Collected Papers*, vol. 2, pp. 294–95.

30. Freud, "Further Recommendations in the Techniques of Psychoanalysis," *Collected Papers*, vol. 2, p. 353.

31. Freud, "Sexuality and Aetiology," *Collected Papers*, vol. 1, p. 239.

32. Freud, "Turnings in the Ways of Psycho-analytic Therapy," *Collected Papers,* vol. 2, pp. 400–01. Cf. *The Question of Lay Analysis,* p. 99.
33. Cited in H.-J. Bannach, "Die wissenschaftliche Bedeuting des alten Berliner Psychoanalytischen Instituts," *Psyche,* XXV (1971), p. 243.
34. *James Jackson Putnam and Psychoanalysis: Letters Between Putnam and Freud,* ed. Nathan G. Hale (Cambridge, Massachusetts, 1971), pp. 90–91 (emphasis added).
35. Freud, "Recommendations for Physicians on the Psycho-analytic Method of Treatment," *Collected Papers,* vol. 2, p. 327.
36. Freud, "Further Recommendations in the Technique of Psychoanalysis," *Collected Papers,* vol. 2, p. 383.
37. That much of contemporary psychoanalysis itself has retreated from Freud's position is shown in Paul Halmos, *The Faith of the Counsellors* (New York, 1970), pp. 94 ff. Halmos cited from recent psychoanalytical literature and comments, "Psychoanalysis has not committed its followers to some of the most fundamental tenets of the theory, namely those which insist that therapy should be reductive so that the patient should be able to resolve the present in terms of the objective insight he gains from the past, and not in terms of either a mystical and spiritual communion with the analyst, or in terms of directions and value-judgments coming from him" (p. 97).
38. Clara Thompson, *Interpersonal Psychoanalysis: The Selected Papers of Clara M. Thompson,* ed. Maurice R. Green, foreword by Erich Fromm (New York, 1964), p. 79. "Since analysis was becoming too intellectualized," Thompson wrote, "Ferenczi sought ways to encourage more emotional reliving" (p. 78). Aside from whether this is a valid interpretation of Ferenczi's contribution, would it be fair to append to this statement on the overintellectualization of psychoanalysis an exchange between Wortis and Freud? Wortis remarked, " 'The Jews are over-intellectualized; it was Jung who said, for example, that psychoanalysis bears the mark of this Jewish over-intellectualization.' 'So much better for psychoanalysis then!' said Freud" (J. Wortis, *Fragments of an Analysis with Freud,* p. 146).
39. Izette de Forest, *The Leaven of Love: A Development of the Psychoanalytic Theory and Technique of Sandor Ferenczi* (Hamden, Connecticut, 1965), p. 15.
40. Fromm, "Die gesellschaftliche Bedingheit der psychoanalytischen

Therapie," *Zeitschrift für Sozialforschung*, IV (1935), p. 391.
41. Cf. Adorno, "Die revidierte Psychoanalyse," in Adorno, Hork-heimer, and Marcuse, *Kritische Theorie der Gesellschaft* (n.p., n.d.), IV, p. 39.
42. Freud, *Civilization and Its Discontents* (New York, 1962), p. 49.
43. Adorno, "Kierkegaards Lehre von der Liebe," in *Kierkegaard* (Frankfurt, 1966), p. 272.
44. Marcuse, "On Hedonism," in *Negations* (Boston, 1968), p. 168.
45. *Ibid.*, p. 166.

VII   Theory and Therapy II: Laing and Cooper

1. I am in partial agreement with Jan B. Gordon, "The Meta-Journey of R. D. Laing," in *R. D. Laing and Anti-Psychiatry*, ed. Robert Boyers (New York, 1971); and Peter Sedgewick, "Mental Illness Is Illness," *Salmagundi*, 20 (1972), pp. 196 ff.
2. R. D. Laing, *Politics of Experience* (Middlesex, England, 1969), p. 95.
3. David Cooper, *Psychiatry and Anti-Psychiatry* (New York, 1971), p. 35.
4. Cooper, *Death of the Family* (New York, 1971), p. 60.
5. *Ibid.*, p. 16.
6. "The investigation of the relation between individuals and society . . . is reduced to the study of the interdependence of individuals and groups" (Frankfurt Institute for Social Research, *Aspects of Sociology* [Boston, 1972], p. 60, and Institut für Sozialforschung, *Soziologische Exkurse* [Frankfurt, 1956], p. 60).
   The diversity of the group dynamic tradition can be glimpsed in one of its advocates, Kurt Lewin. First, evident in his writings is an existential moment, protesting against a narrow behaviorism which abstracts the individual from a human context: "One of the basic characteristics of field theory in psychology . . . is the demand that the field that influences an individual should be described not in 'objective physicalistic' terms, but in the way in which it exists for that person at that time." But, as with Laing and Cooper, this in no way precludes the mathematization or formalization of this context: "It is possible to determine and to measure psychological atmospheres quite accurately" (Kurt Lewin, *Field Theory in Social Science*, ed. Dorwin Cartwright [New York, 1951, 1964], pp. 62–63). Secondly, Lewin was an

initiator and organizer of the first T-groups and sensitivity training (see Alfred J. Marrow, *The Practical Theorist: The Life and Work of Kurt Lewin* [New York, 1969], pp. 210 ff). Finally, it could be noted that Lewin was a lifelong friend of Karl Korsch — which perhaps explains or is explained by the positivist bent in Korsch's own thought; Lewin wrote a pamphlet in 1920 on Taylorism in a series edited by Korsch on "Practical Socialism." They also collaborated on a paper in 1939 on "Mathematical Constructs in Psychology and Sociology."

7. R. D. Laing and Aaron Esterson, *Sanity, Madness and the Family* (New York, 1964), pp. 7, 9.

8. *Ibid.*, p. 13 (emphasis in the original). Or less flamboyantly: "The most significant theoretical and methodological development in psychiatry of the last two decades is, in my view, the growing dissatisfaction with any theory or study of the individual which isolates him from his context (Laing, *Self and Others* [New York, 1969], 2nd rev. ed., p. 65).

9. Laing, *Sanity, Madness and the Family*, p. 59.

10. *Ibid.*, p. 83.

11. Laing, *The Politics of the Family* (New York, 1971), p. 49.

12. *Ibid.*, p. 48.

13. Laing, Herbert Phillipson, and A. Russell Lee, *Interpersonal Perception* (New York, 1972), p. 172.

14. Aaron Esterson, *The Leaves of Spring: Schizophrenia, Family and Sacrifice* (Middlesex, England, 1972), p. 243.

15. Cf. August Hollingshead and Fredrick C. Redlich, *Social Class and Mental Illness* (New York, 1967), and Jerome K. Meyers and Bertram H. Roberts, *Family and Class Dynamics in Mental Illness* (New York, 1964).

16. Laing, *The Politics of the Family*, pp. 41–42.

17. For a recent bibliography of this material see *The Politics of Health Care*, eds. Ken Rosenberg and Gordon Schiff, Boston Medical Committee for Human Rights (Boston, n.d.).

18. For a survey of occupational accidents and diseases see F. Wallick, *The American Worker: An Endangered Species* (New York, 1972).

19. See Rodger Hurley, "The Health Crisis of the Poor," and, in the same volume, Charles C. Hughes and John M. Hunter, "Disease and 'Development' in Africa," in *Social Organization of Health*, ed. Hans Peter Dreitzel (New York, 1971).

20. Laing et al., *Interpersonal Perception*, p. 8. Cf. David Cooper,

"Freud Revisited," *New Left Review*, 20 (Summer 1963), pp. 112 ff.

21. Cooper, *Psychiatry and Anti-Psychiatry*, p. 29.
22. Laing, *The Politics of the Family*, p. 46.
23. Gregory Bateson, "Towards a Theory of Schizophrenia," in Bateson, *Steps to an Ecology of Mind* (New York, 1972), pp. 205, 206.
24. To be sure, the intent is exactly to undo the "knots" or the spirals of mis-communication. "The patterns delineated here have not yet been classified by a Linnaeus of human bondage" (Laing, *Knots* [New York, 1970], p. i). But this intent is concerned with the failures of communication; it does not turn into a critique of this mode of communication in general.
25. Laing et al., *Interpersonal Perception*, p. 30.
26. *Ibid.*, p. 36.
27. "We have all noticed those people attracted to plate glass windows, transported by their own reflection in the glass. Caught by their own glance, they are compelled to see themselves the way Others see them. A perpetual rhythm etched into the hardened surfaces of the urbanized world, reflecting the Image Crisis that affects all of those who must define themselves in relation to the Super-Alien Other. On all sides these mirrors beckon and insist" (Maxy Beml, "William Burroughs and the Invisible Generation," *Telos*, 13 (Fall 1972), p. 129.
28. Laing, *Self and Others*, p. 157.
29. Other humanist psychologists have combined with apparent ease a humanist approach with a positivist one. With Harry Stack Sullivan the stress on interpersonal relations coexisted with operationalism. Sullivan himself was influenced by an operationalist theorist, Percy W. Bridgman, and at one time gave an "operationalist" subtitle to his journal *Psychiatry* (see the remarks by Sullivan's editor, Helen Swick Perry, in Sullivan, *Fusion of Psychiatry and Social Science* [New York, 1971]). Cf. Martin Birnbach, *Neo-Freudian Social Philosophy* (Stanford, California, 1961), pp. 58 ff.
30. Laing, *The Divided Self* (Baltimore, 1965), p. 10.
31. For a Marcusian critique of Sartre, see Ronald Aronson, "The Roots of Sartre's Thought," *Telos*, 13 (1972), pp. 47 ff; and for a somewhat different presentation of the existential moment in Laing, see Carl Ratner, "Principles of Dialectical Psychology," *Telos*, 9 (1971), especially pp. 98 ff.

32. Laing et al., *Interpersonal Perception*, pp. 3, 4.
33. Sidney Hook, *From Hegel to Marx* (Ann Arbor, 1962), p. 258.
34. Ludwig Feuerbach, *Principles of the Philosophy of the Future*, ed. Manfred H. Vogel (New York, 1966), pp. 71–72.
35. The fragment is found in the appendix to Karl Marx and Fried-rich Engels, *The German Ideology* (Moscow, 1964), p. 660.
36. *Ibid.*, p. 58.
37. Marx, "Theses on Feuerbach," VI, *ibid.*, p. 652.
38. Herbert Marcuse, *Studies in Critical Philosophy* (Boston, 1973), p. 21.
39. For a discussion of the concept of labor, see Marcuse, "Über die philosophischen Grundlagen des wirtschaftswissenschaftlichen Arbeitsbegriff," in Marcuse, *Kultur und Gesellschaft*, II (Frankfurt, 1965). An English translation is now in *Telos*, 16 (Summer 1973).
40. Marcuse, "The Foundations of Historical Materialism," p. 22.
41. Laing et al., *Interpersonal Perception*, p. 6.
42. "The spectacle within society corresponds to the concrete manu-facture of alienation" (Guy Debord, *Society of the Spectacle* [Detroit, 1970], p. 30).
43. Norman O. Brown, "A Reply to Herbert Marcuse," in Marcuse, *Negations* (Boston, 1968), p. 244.
44. Theodor W. Adorno, *Minima Moralia* (Frankfurt, 1964), p. 323.
45. See Adorno's "The Stars Down to Earth: The *Los Angeles Times'* Astrology Column," in *Jahrbuch für Amerikastudien*, II (1957), pp. 19 ff.
46. Ira Progoff, *The Death and Rebirth of Psychology* (New York, 1956).
47. Adorno, *Minima Moralia*, p. 118.

Index

185